# Harry Styles

# AS IT IS

## The Illustrated Biography

Carolyn McHugh

BOOKS

## sona
BOOKS

First published in the U.K. 2021 as Harry Styles Adore you. This is a fully revised and updated edition.

CAT NO: SON0559

**Photography courtesy of**

**Getty images:**

- Anthony Pham
- Bo Kallberg/PYMCA-Avalon/Universal Images Group
- Borrelli/Chicago Tribune/Tribune News Service
- Brian Rasic
- Chris Hyde
- Christopher Polk
- Dave J Hogan
- Dia Dipasupil
- Don Arnold/WireImage
- Eamonn McCormack/WireImage
- FOX Image Collection
- FRANCOIS LO PRESTI/AFP
- Fred Dufour/AFP
- FREDERIC J. BROWN/AFP

- Gilbert Carrasquillo
- Isaac Brekken
- James Flood/Comic Relief
- Jason LaVeris/FilmMagic
- JB Lacroix/WireImage
- Jeff Kravitz/FilmMagic for Sony Music
- JMEnternational
- John Lamparski/WireImage
- John Shearer/WireImage
- Jon Kopaloff/FilmMagic/WireImage
- Joseph Okpako/WireImage
- Karwai Tang/WireImage
- Kevin Mazur/MG19
- Kevin Winter
- Laurent Koffel/Gamma-Rapho

- Laurent Viteur/WireImage
- Mark Holloway/Redferns
- Mat Hayward
- Matt Winkelmeyer/MG19
- MEGA/GC Images
- Mike Coppola/WireImage
- Mike Marsland/WireImage
- Rich Fury
- Scott Dudelson/WireImage
- Scott Legato
- Steve Jennings/WireImage
- Suzi Pratt/WireImage
- Terence Patrick/CBS
- Theo Wargo
- Tiziana FABI / AFP

**Wiki Commoms:**

- Cedrick Jones

Book layout & design: Darren Grice at Ctrl-d
Copy editors: Tom O'Neill / Juliette O'Neill

Made in EU.
ISBN 978-1-915343-19-2

# Contents

Harry Styles is a modern phenomenon — one of the most influential artists in music today – he was a superstar musician and multi-millionaire before he was 20.

Since first finding fame aged 16 as a member of One Direction, one of the biggest boy bands of all time, he has risen above all his contemporaries to become a respected solo artist. Now he's a feted singer/songwriter/performer, an actor, a fashionista and a 21st century casanova with a £75 million fortune amassed along his fun-filled way.

Endlessly fascinating to his fans and commentators alike, he is rarely out of the headlines. Sometimes it's for professional reasons, such as his music or movies, but other times for more frivolous topics such as his hair or his love life.

8

But he handles the whole showbiz shebang with his famous charm and grace as...

...he's one of the good guys.

## The Style Files

Full Name: Harry Edward Styles

Born: 1 February 1994

Star Sign: Aquarius

First Word: Cat

Childhood Pet: Max, a grey-speckled border collie/lurcher cross, with a curly tail and multicoloured eyes

First Job: Saturday boy at the W Mandeville Bakery in Holmes Chapel

9

# Hello Harry

## His early years, growing up, first band

Harry's journey from obscurity to superstardom began in the Worcestershire town of Evesham, UK. He was born on 1 February 1994, baby brother to three-year-old sister Gemma.

His parents, Anne Twist and Desmond Styles, moved the family to Holmes Chapel in Cheshire a few years later and that's where Harry grew up. He famously described the place as 'quite boring – picturesque' during his X Factor audition.

Harry always describes his childhood as a happy one and credits his parents as always being hugely loving and supportive. However he does remember crying when his parents told him they were splitting up in 2001, when he was just seven years old. He and his sister remained living with their mother, who married her partner of 10 years Robin Twist in 2013, providing Harry with step siblings Amy and Mike Twist. Harry was best man at Anne and Robin's wedding. Sadly, Robin died of cancer in 2017.

Harry has also remained very close to his father who was a huge music fan and introduced him to classic artists including Elvis, The Beatles, Pink Floyd and Queen. Harry showed an interest in music from a very early age. As well as liking the rock enjoyed by his father, he also enjoyed music by his mother's favourite, Shania Twain. Fleetwood Mac was another family favourite. 'In my family, we listened at home, we listened in the car, we listened wherever we could. Dreams was the first song I knew all the words to, before I even knew what the words meant', Harry said years later when he had the surreal experience of inducting Fleetwood Mac legend Stevie Nicks into the Rock and Roll Hall of Fame.

He made good use of a present from his grandfather of a karaoke machine, with Handbags and Gladrags by Rod Stewart, one of his favourites to perform in his bedroom.

In an article for Another Man magazine, Harry's sister Gemma remembers him as a loud and boisterous little boy whose incredible charm was evident even then.

'When I started school in Holmes Chapel, on hot days when the school-run cars were lined up outside and the parents were passing the time, Harry — never scared of attracting attention — would be stood up in the back of the car, entertaining everyone through the open window. Even then he had that sort of magnetism that made people just want to watch him. He made people laugh. Babies still tend to stare at him now — it's kind of weird.'

He always found it easy to make friends and on one family holiday to Cyprus, aged about seven, could be found each morning holding court around the pool with people three times his age. 'When we left on a shuttle bus back to the airport at the end of our trip there was a crowd of young adult women gathered on the pavement waving him off through the window, shouting their goodbyes', said Gemma. 'Sometimes I look at him now and wonder how he manages to entrance people, skipping about just being himself, but actually he's always done it — only now more people get to watch.'

11

# He was well-liked by pupils and staff alike at his school Holmes Chapel Comprehensive and enjoyed life there.

Not long before leaving school Harry formed a rock-pop band with school friends. Called White Eskimo, and with Harry as lead singer, the band did reasonably well, winning a local Battle of the Bands competition and performing a few gigs at parties and weddings. Harry wrote his first song, called Winter, at this time — he now describes it as 'not the best'.

'He was a joker, talkative and very distracting', says Gemma. But he did ok in his GCSEs and was set to go to sixth form to take A levels in law, sociology and business when his life suddenly turned in a completely different direction.

# If at first you don't succeed

## Harry's time on The X Factor

Harry first came to public attention when he auditioned for a place on the seventh series of the UK's massive Saturday night talent show, The X Factor, in 2010. Encouraged by his mum Anne, who first put him forward for the competition, 16-year-old Harry was surprised to get through to the televised auditions.

Sister Gemma remembers that's when things suddenly felt real. 'There's a list of songs that contestants select from and we pored over it to choose ones that he already knew, ones he liked and ones he couldn't imagine singing.'

'When he had to practice, he suddenly became shy and wouldn't let us listen. He was constantly singing before and, at first, I didn't understand why this was any different. After a lot of persuasion, he would stand in the bathroom with the door shut and sing Isn't She Lovely and Hey, Soul Sister, while Mum and I sat on the landing outside.'

Harry's first audition was in Manchester, in front of regular judges music mogul Simon Cowell and boy band supremo Louis Walsh. The third judge was usually singer Cheryl Cole, but she was away when Harry auditioned and so former Pussy Cat Doll singer Nicole Scherzinger stood in.

Talking to the camera ahead of his first appearance before the judges, Harry explained that the success of his school-boy band White Eskimo, winning Battle of the Bands at school and playing to that many people, had shown him that it was what he wanted to do. 'I got such a thrill when I was in front of people singing, it made me want to do it more and more. People tell me that I'm a good singer — but it's usually my mum'.

Harry's parents Anne and Des were shown on camera, watching proudly from behind the scenes wearing 'We think Harry has the X Factor' t-shirts' as their son sang the Stevie Wonder hit, 'Isn't She Lovely', a capella in a confident audition which was to change his life forever.

Dressed casually in a white top and grey cardigan, with a long patterned scarf wound around his neck, Harry won over the live audience and gained a 'Yes, through to the next round' from Simon and Nicole. 'For 16-years-old you have a beautiful voice', said Nicole. Only Louis had reservations at that stage, saying 'no' to sending Harry through to the next round, explaining that he felt Harry was 'so young' and lacking experience. Simon said Louis was talking 'rubbish' and told Harry '...I think with a bit of vocal coaching you actually could be very good.'

Luckily for Harry, the two 'yes' votes from Nicole and Simon were enough to get him through to the next stage — the Bootcamp audition in London. Gemma travelled with Harry to Wembley Arena where a small crowd was gathering outside. 'Everyone looked so much older than him and people were dotted around in small groups, posturing and harmonising, and generally sussing out the competition. He spotted a young guy he'd chatted to at a previous audition and I realised it was time to leave him, 16 years old, and in the shadows of a building we'd only seen on TV.

'I stayed nearby so that when the call came and he was out of the competition, I could go and commiserate, take him home to Cheshire and school, and back to his normal life. None of us wanted him to fail but we never dreamed things would go the way they did. That call never came. He has just kept on winning and winning — maybe not The X Factor, but there's no denying he's golden. My baby brother never came home again. He grew up, and all of our memories became his origin story.'

But his journey wasn't without its ups and downs. Initially Harry was eliminated from the solo competition during the 'bootcamp' stage and shown leaving the stage visibly upset. However there was to be an 11th hour reprieve. Entries for the 'Groups' category were considered weak that year, so the producers hit on the idea of putting together a couple of bands, using eliminated contestants who had initially auditioned as soloists.

Harry was among those chosen to join the new boy band, along with four other soon-to-be household names, Liam Payne, Niall Horan, Louis Tomlinson and Zayn Malik. Harry is credited as coming up with their band name — One Direction.

The group went through to the 'Judge's Houses' stage — travelling to Marbella in Spain to perform for Simon, who was mentoring the 'Groups' category, and guest judge Sinitta. They sang the Natalie Imbruglia hit Torn but were under-rehearsed and nervous.

However they got through, with Simon telling them; 'My head is saying this is a risk, and my heart is saying you deserve a shot, and that's why it's been difficult. Guys I've made a decision, I've gone with my heart. You're through'. .

On to the live tv shows and the boys were popular from the start. They were a standout act in what is now considered one of the strongest ever series of the show, which was ITV's Saturday night highlight between 9 October and 12 December 2010.

One Direction proved firm fan favourites, with Harry in particular making his mark and getting a lot of camera time.

By all accounts he was great fun behind the scenes too — the life and soul of X Factor that year.

One Direction progressed week by week to the final, eventually finishing in third position, behind Rebecca Ferguson and the eventual winner Matt Cardle. But their finishing position didn't matter. The whole series had been a great shop window for them. The final itself was watched by 17.7 million people, making it the highest rated show of 2010 and eventually the entire decade, in the UK.

So their failure to triumph on the night mattered not a jot. They had amassed a huge fan base and, crucially, their mentor Simon Cowell felt they were absolutely what he needed to fill a gap in the music market for a boy band. As he spent a lot of his time in the US, Simon had spotted a hunger for a band to challenge the (at the time) mighty Justin Bieber and his 'Belieber' fans. The showbiz world was itching for some new faces to come through .

So he signed the band to his SyCo label in a deal said at the time to be worth up to £2million. 'I think they've all got potential', said Simon. 'It's now down to how much they want it. They've all got talent.'

'Singing is what I want to do and if people who can make that happen for me don't think that I should be doing that, then it's a major setback in my plans.'

Harry speaking before his X Factor audition in 2010.

15

⌐ ¬ Harry Styles attends the world premiere of Harry
Potter and The Deathly Hallows at Odeon Leicester
Square, London — 11 November, 2010

# Headed in the right direction

## the One Direction years

Their youthful good looks and bright pop/rock sound made One Direction one of the biggest and best-selling boy bands of all time. Pitched perfectly to delight legions of teenage female fans, who became known as 'Directioners', the band chalked up hit after hit between 2011 and 2015. Every member of the band amassed a personal fortune and became a worldwide celebrity.

Since 2010, and having been on an indefinite hiatus since 2016, 1D has sold 70 million records worldwide, picking up more than 200 awards along the way. Their trophy shelf includes four MTV Video Music Awards, six Billboard Music Awards, seven Brit Awards, seven American Music Awards, and 28 Teen Choice Awards.

16

In 2013, they earned an estimated $75 million and were rated by Forbes magazine as the second highest-earning celebrity act under the age of 30. By 2016 they were ranked as the second highest-earning celebrities in the world, of any age.

Post X Factor, the anticipation of One Direction's future career was huge. The programme famously takes its finalists on a live tour around the UK after the series has finished. For many of the artists involved it is the peak of their career, but for One Direction, their performances on the tour from 19 February to 9 April 2011, served merely as a warm-up for their forthcoming world domination.

Their first single, the buoyant, up-tempo 'What Makes You Beautiful' was released on 11 September 2011 following a massive teaser promotional campaign which generated a record for the most pre-orders for any release that year.

The single was a huge hit, making its debut at # 1 on the UK singles chart and #4 on the

# Introducing One Direction

## Members of One Direction also known as 1D:

### Harry Styles

Born 1 February 1994,
Holmes Chapel, England

### Zayn Malik

Born January 12 1993
Bradford, England

### Niall Horan

Born 13 September 1993,
County Westmeath, Ireland

### Louis Tomlinson

Born 24 December 1991,
Doncaster, England

### Liam Payne

Born 29 August 1993,
Wolverhampton, England

Harry Styles AS IT IS

⌞⌝ Harry Styles signs autographs while visiting
Glasgow, Manchester and London — 11 Sep. 2011

19

Harry Styles AS IT IS

L-R Liam Payne, Louis Tomlinson, Harry Styles, Zayn Malik and Niall Horan of One Direction travel in a luxury helicopter to Glasgow, Manchester and London —
11 September, 2011

US Billboard Hot 100. It went on to top charts around the world and won a 2012 Brit Award for British Single of the Year. By 2016 the song had sold 4.8 million copies in the US, making it a quadruple platinum success. The accompanying video showing the boys having fun in the sun on a beach in California has been viewed more than 1.4 billion times.

Later that year came their debut album  Up All Night, comprising track after track of happy harmonies, was issued on 11 November 2011. It made its debut at # 2 on the UK album chart and became the UK's fast-selling debut album that year. The album also made #1 in the States on the US Billboard 100 chart, selling 176,000 copies in the first week alone.

So began five amazing years which saw 1D conquer the world. Cracking the American market

| Studio albums | Released | Worldwide sales* |
| --- | --- | --- |
| Up All Night | 18 November 2011 | 5.8 million |
| Take Me Home | 9 November 2012 | 5.9 million |
| Midnight Memories | 25 November 2013 | 5.7 million |
| Four | 17 November 2014 | 3.2 million |
| Made in the A.M | 13 November 2015 | 3.3 million |

*as at March 2023

is notoriously tricky for UK acts and many of the biggest stars in their homeland fail to make it across the Atlantic. The fact that the 1D boys made it stateside is testament to their hard work and huge appeal. They were also lucky in that their career correlated with the phenomenal rise in social media platforms from 2010. There's no doubt that a skilful social media campaign from the very start of their career, providing fans with content and fun, massively improved the odds of their succeeding.

# One Direction Singles

What Makes You Beautiful.

Gotta Be You

One More Thing

More Than This

Live While We're Young

Little Things

Kiss You

One Way or Another (Teenage Kicks)

Best Song Ever

Story of My Life

Midnight Memories

You & I

23

Steal My Girl

Night Changes

Drag Me Down

Perfect

History

⌐⌐ One Direction, return to The X Factor stage for the world debut performance of their single, "Story of My Life." — 21 Nov, 2013

In February 2011 the band published a book 'One Direction : Forever Young' which gave a first-hand account of their X Factor story and topped the Sunday Times' Best Seller List.

24

Harry Styles of One Direction performs on stage in
Brisbane, Australia — 18 April, 2012

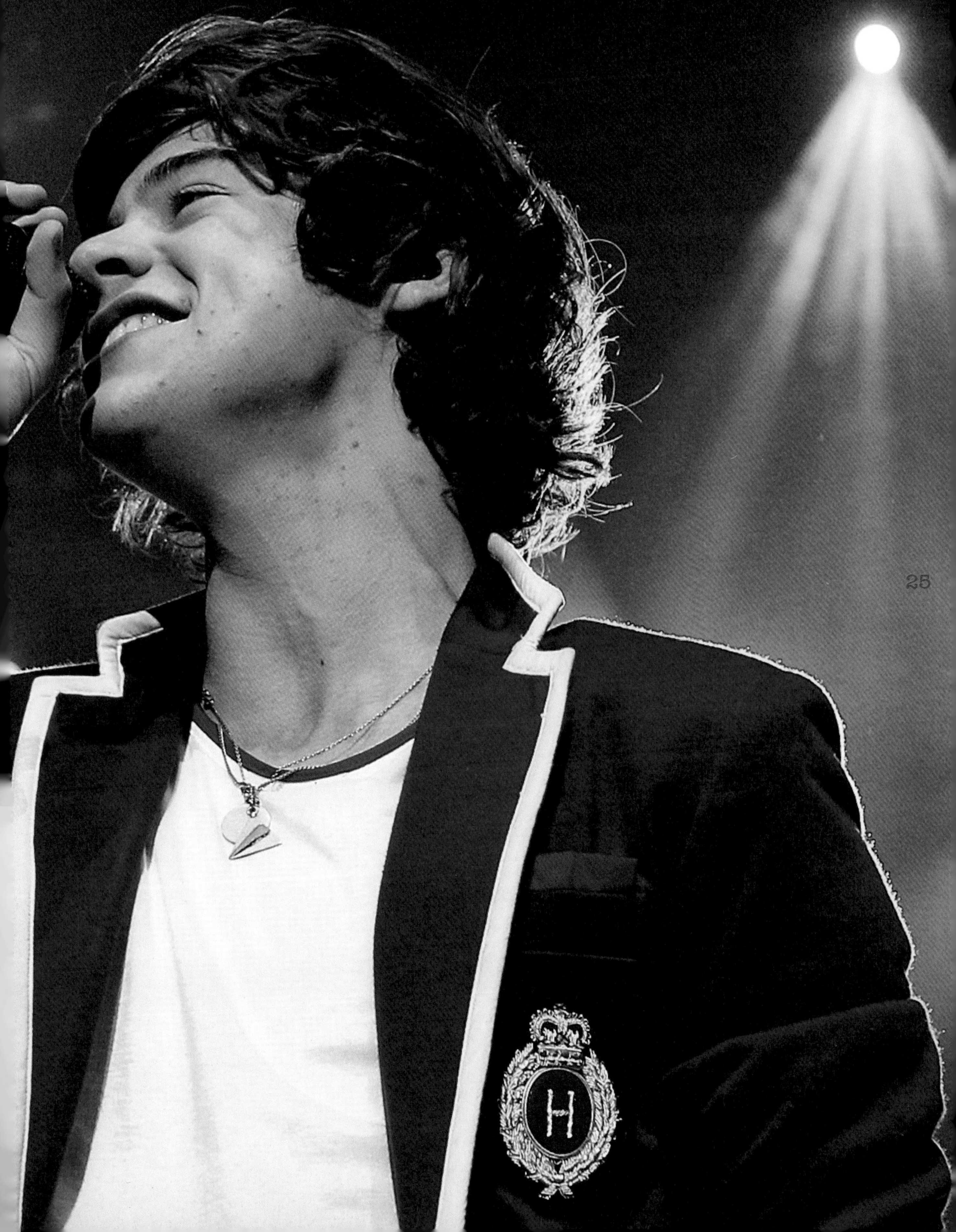

# One Direction tours

## The band were acclaimed live performers, their stage presence was phenomenal, and their live vocals were on point.

### Up All Night
#### 2011-12

Comprising 54 shows across the UK and Ireland, then extended to take in Australia and North American dates.

### Take Me Home
#### 2013

Consisting of 123 shows in Europe, North America, Asia, and Oceania. 300,000 tickets were sold within a day of release in the UK and Ireland, including a six-date sell-out at London's O2 Arena.

### Where We Are
#### 2014

The first all stadium tour kicking off in Columbia on 25 April to 5 October in Florida, and taking in dates throughout South America, UK and Europe and North America. It was the highest grossing tour of the year and the highest grossing tour of all time by a vocal group.

### On The Road Again
#### 2015

2.3 million tickets for 80 shows in Australia, Asia, Africa, Europe, and North America. Grossing $208 million.

[ ] Harry Styles of One Direction in the press room at the 2014 American Music Awards at Nokia Theatre LA. Live, Los Angeles, California — 23 November, 2014

27

1D was named Global Recording Artist of 2013 by the International Federation of the Phonographic Industry; Billboard Artist of the Year 2014 and American Music Awards Artist of the Year in 2014 and 2015

28

One Direction perform onstage during the 2012 MTV Video
Music Awards in Los Angeles, California — 06 Sep, 2012

29

30

## Up All Night typical set list

1. Na Na Na
2. Stand Up
3. I Wish
4. **Medley:** I Gotta Feeling/Stereo Hearts/ Valerie/ Torn
5. Moments
6. Gotta Be You
7. More Than This
8. Up All Night
9. Tell Me a Lie
10. Everything About You
11. Use Somebody
12. One Thing
13. Save You Tonight
14. What Makes You Beautiful

**2012**

The new year found 1D one month into the UK leg of their very first concert tour, Up All Night. Having kicked off in December 2011, 1D were on the road until July 2012, taking in North America, Canada, Mexico, Australia and New Zealand.

A DVD of their appearance in Bournemouth 'Up All Night: The Live Tour' was released in May 2012 and topped the charts in 25 countries.

In November 2012 1D released their second album Take Me Home, including the exuberant hit single Live While We're Young. The album notched up the highest one-week opening sales figures by a non-US artist in America. It was the fastest-selling album of the year and made # 1 in 32 countries.

Fans also went 'crazy, crazy crazy' for the Live While We're Young video which showed the band waking up in a tent and then having a ball at a music festival, wet and bare-chested by the final scenes. It was viewed 8.4 million times within a 24-hour period just after its release and went on to get 26.1 million hits on YouTube.

In reality the boys were a long way away from the lives of regular festival-goers, having begun to enjoy a jet-set lifestyle as their success grew. Solidifying their position as the new princes of pop, the band also performed 'What Makes You Beautiful' at the closing ceremony of the London Olympics that year. It was a huge honour for the young band, as only the cream of British culture at the time was chosen to fly the flag for the UK in its Olympic shows which were broadcast around the world.

31

BBC Radio 1's Teen Awards, Wembley Arena
London, UK — 07 Oct. 2012

2013

With 'Directioners' at fever pitch all over the world, the band could do no wrong in 2013. The band spent most of the year on the road on their 'Take Me Home' tour which began in London on 23 February and was frequently extended to take in Europe, North America and Australia before concluding in Japan on 3 November.

'It's insane that people want to see us,' said Harry. But they did. In fact the hysteria from fans was reminiscent of that surrounding The Beatles, who broke the boy band market 50 years before them.

The group also released a concert-tour documentary, 'One Direction: This Is Us' — a fly-on-the-wall, access-all-areas look at life on the road. As well as including live concert footage filmed at the O2 in London from the Take Me Home tour, the film also featured footage showing background concert preparation, as well as profiling the five band member's lives before they joined One Direction and enjoyed their meteoric rise to worldwide fame. Directed by Morgan Spurlock, the film was a massive hit at the box office, grossing over six times its budget for makers Sony.

At the end of the year, on 25 November, the band released its third studio album, Midnight Memories. The album was testament to the fact that the band had 'grown up' since its X Factor days. Tracks were less 'pop' with more of a 'rock' feel and slightly edgier lyrically. The Daily Telegraph's review said; 'It is all so swaggeringly confident and honed to a perfect point, it is hard not to be caught up in its own sense of conviction'. AllMusic decided; 'when the album ends and the various styles, songs and moods are added up, Midnight Memories ends up as another satisfying album that does everything a One D album should do and then some.'

'And then some' indeed — it sold four million copies worldwide within five weeks of its release and went on to become the best-selling album in the world that year.

1D became the first band to have its first four albums debut at #1 in the US and the first band in the US to land two #1 albums in the same calendar year (2012).

32

[ ] Harry Styles performs onstage at the "One Direction iHeartRadio Album Release Party" hosted by Ryan Seacrest at the iHeartRadio Theater Los Angeles

## Take Me Home typical set list

1. Up All Night
2. I Would
3. Heart Attack
4. More Than This
5. Loved You First
6. One Thing
7. C'mon, C'mon
8. Change My Mind
9. One Way or Another/Teenage Kicks
10. Last First Kiss
11. Moments
12. Back For You
13. Summer Love
14. Over Again
15. Little Things
16. Teenage Dirtbag
17. Rock Me
18. She's Not Afraid
19. Kiss You
20. Live While We're Young
21. What Makes You Beautiful

[ ] One Direction attend a book signing for their book 'Where
We Are' at Alexandra Palace, London — 18 November, 2013

## Where We Are
## typical set list

1. Midnight Memories
2. Little Black Dress
3. Kiss You
4. Why Don't We Go There?
5. Rock Me
6. Don't Forget Where You Belong
7. Live While We're Young
8. C'mon, C'mon
9. Right Now
10. Through the Dark
11. Happily
12. Little Things
13. Moments
14. Strong
15. Better Than Words
16. Alive
17. One Thing
18. Diana
19. What Makes You Beautiful
20. You and I
21. Story of My Life
22. Little White Lies
23. Best Song Ever

The mammoth 1D machine rolled on as the boys continued making and selling hit records and concert tickets in 2014.

There was a huge hunger for their music and merchandise, which merged perfectly as they embarked on their first all-stadium world tour, 'Where We Are'. In support of their third album, Midnight Memories, the tour was seen by almost 3.5 million people and made over $290 million, making it the highest-grossing concert tour of that year. It is also the highest-grossing tour by a vocal group in history. Kicking off in Columbia on 25 April, the tour took to North and South America, Europe and the UK.

There was another biography One Direction: Who We Are was another Sunday Times best-seller, published in September 2014.

They released their album 'Four' — so named as it was their fourth album and fourth year as a band — on 17 November. It was another huge success, selling 3.2 million copies and topping the charts in 18 countries, including the UK. Debuting at # 1 on the US Billboard 200 album chart, the album gave 1D another first — as the first band in the chart's 58-year history to have its first four albums all enter at number one.

37

[ ] One Direction perform onstage at the 2014 American Music Awards at Nokia Theatre L.A. Live — 23 November, 2014

Although the five boys undoubtedly had fun, their hectic schedule must have taken its toll. Producing an album a year, accompanying videos and undertaking four tours in five years meant that the pace was relentless and the schedule insane. Alongside the music came a succession of promotional events, tv appearances, not to mention their arduous travel schedule.

The cracks began to show shortly after the band embarked on another world stadium tour, 'On The Road Again'. This ran from 7 February 2015 in Sydney, Australia, until 31 October 2015 in Sheffield, England, taking in Asia, Africa, Australia and Europe to become the second highest-grossing tour of the year. But its success was marred when, less than two months in, Zayn suddenly left the group. His final appearance with the group – and the band's last as a quintet – was at the AsiaWorld Arena in Hong Kong on 18 March.

Fans were stunned by the news, particularly because any speculation around such an event had usually centred on Harry leaving the group.

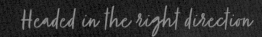 Harry Styles of One Direction performs on stage at CenturyLink Field, Seattle, Washington — 15 July, 2015

39

## On The Road Again
## typical set list

1. Clouds
2. Steal My Girl
3. Where Do Broken Hearts Go
4. Midnight Memories
5. Kiss You
6. Ready to Run
7. Happily
8. Strong
9. Better Than Words
10. Don't Forget Where You Belong
11. Little Things
12. Night Changes
13. Alive
14. Diana
15. One Thing
16. What Makes You Beautiful
17. Through the Dark
18. Girl Almighty
19. The Story of My Life
20. You & I
21. Little White Lies
22. Little Black Dress
23. Best Song Ever

In a statement about his departure, Zayn said; 'My life with One Direction has been more than I could ever have imagined. But, after five years, I feel like it is now the right time for me to leave the band. I'd like to apologise to the fans if I've let anyone down, but I have to do what feels right in my heart. I am leaving because I want to be a normal 22-year-old who is able to relax and have some private time out of the spotlight. I know I have four friends for life in Louis, Liam, Harry and Niall. I know they will continue to be the best band in the world.'

For their part, the band said; 'We're really sad to see Zayn go, but we totally respect his decision and send him all our love for the future. The past five years have been beyond amazing, we've gone through so much together, so we will always be friends. The four of us will now continue. We're looking forward to recording the new album and seeing all the fans on the next stage of the world tour.'

The band made its first official public appearance as a four-piece on James Corden's Late Late Show in the USA that May and confirmed that they were not seeking a new fifth member to replace Zayn. In fact between themselves privately they had already decided to call it a day and midway through the tour announced they would be taking an '18-month hiatus', which later turned into an indefinite hiatus.

Before disbanding they finished the tour and went on to make a fifth album Made in the A.M., released 13 November. It debuted at #1 in the UK and at #2 in the US, selling 2.4 million copies worldwide at the time. But the air of finality was unmistakeable. The group's final show was at the UK's Sheffield Arena on 31 October, 2015.

In true 1D style, the band undoubtedly went out on a high. Rolling Stone magazine described Made in the A.M. as being, '1D's Let It Be — the kind of record the world's biggest pop group makes when it's time to say thanks for the memories. The cover has Beatles-worthy coded body language: four boys on a cheap dorm couch, Liam Payne and Niall Horan smiling in opposite directions, Louis Tomlinson and Harry Styles staring defiantly into your eyes. Lots of sensitive breakup songs here

"I love the band and would never rule out anything in the
future. The band changed my life, gave me everything."
Harry on rumours of a 1D reunion.

41

[ ] Harry Styles performs in support of the On The Road Again Tour at Ford Field, Detroit, Michigan — 29 August, 2015

42

– hey, girl, before you go, let's toast the minibars and expensive cars, the good champagne and private planes.'

The final track on the album, and the band's final single release was called 'History' – certainly a fitting title as the band had made sure of its own place in the music history books.

By the time they took their final bows, the boys of One Direction had sold 20.98 million records in the UK alone.

In an interview with Rolling Stone magazine Harry explained that the four remaining members decided to take a break so as not to exhaust their fan base.

'If you're short-sighted you can think, "Let's just keep touring" but we all thought too much of the group to let that happen. You realise you're exhausted, and you don't want to drain people's belief in you'.

43

Their fans were devastated though – flooding social media platforms in a mass out-pouring of grief. But they didn't have too long to wait before each member re-emerged with a solo project. Harry in particular had lots of ideas, charisma, swagger and talent. The music world waited to see if he really would, as predicted, become the breakout international star from the band ......

[ ] Harry Styles of One Direction performs on stage at CenturyLink Field, Seattle, Washington — 15 July, 2015

45

# Striking out
## Harry's life as a solo artist

Once One Direction had said its goodbyes, it was generally considered more a question of 'when' not 'if' Harry would release his own material.

While the life of a solo artist is, as Jay Z said, very different from that of a band member, Harry was really up for the change, telling Rolling Stone magazine; 'When I was in the band I was constantly scared I might sing a wrong note. I felt so much weight in terms of not getting things wrong. I remember when I signed my record deal I asked my manager, "what happens if I get arrested? Does it mean the contract is null and void?"

'Now I feel like the fans have given me an environment to be myself and grow up and create this safe space to learn and make mistakes.'

46

Matt McCardle, who beat 1D on The X Factor, said;' I think it was a brave move to not even try to transition from the boy band sound and to just do what he wanted to do.'

But fame in a boy band is no guarantee of solo success. Many have tried and failed. But few people had any doubts that Harry would make the grade. Harry had already begun writing songs for other artists while he was still in 1D. Back in 2014 he was credited with writing the love ballad Just A Little Bit of Your Heart for Ariana Grande's album My Everything. 'The first time I heard it I was so like, touched, and moved, it was beautiful', said Ariana

During the hiatus between the band and his own solo releases, Harry continued his collaborations with other songwriters, doubtless honing his skills.

In an interview with the Press Association, Johnny McDaid of the rock band Snow

Everything he does seems to be effortless, even now, watching him leap around a stage in front of thousands of people he seems untroubled and free from self-doubt. Its easy to be jealous — he's one of those people who are just good at things, we all know one — but to assume this means he takes it all for granted, or doesnt worry, or try, would be oversimplifying him unfairly. His bundles of talent are a mixture of natural ability and intense heart. Harry's sister Gemma, speaking about her brother's natural charisma.

Patrol said he'd been collaborating with Harry 'for years ..... I think the world is going to be really shocked at what he comes up with. I'm really excited by the way he's sounding at the minute, he's such a talent.'

Then in May 2016, Ryan Tedder, front man of OneRepublic confirmed that he was also writing with Harry. And Meghan Trainor worked with Harry on the track Someday for Michael Bublé's' Nobody But Me album and described him as, 'unbelievable ...he's a very, very talented songwriter... I was very impressed.'

48

But all the while Harry's eye was on the prize of a successful solo career for himself

His first solo album, simply self-titled Harry Styles, was eagerly anticipated and did not disappoint.

Released in May 2017, the 10-track debut album was a huge success, selling 230,000 plus copies within the first week of its release in May 2017.

Speaking to Howard Stern in the States, Harry said he thought he'd 'got lucky' with his recording contract. 'I have to say ....Rob Stringer, who's the head of Sony, he signed me — he signed us in the band as well so I've been with him for a while — but when I signed on my own I said, I kind of need to go and like figure this out a little bit and I'm not going to be able to do it if you're breathing down my neck basically. And he was amazing about it, he said; 'I want to hear it when you're ready to play it to me. So go and do your thing and when you're ready I'll hear it'.

His boss didn't hear the album until it was finished. It was probably rather nerve-wracking, but ultimately was clearly a good decision. The album has gone on to sell 1.325 million physical copies all over the world with streaming figures still rising.

In support of the eponymous album, Harry set off on his first solo tour, selling close to one million tickets for 89 sell-out shows across Europe, North and South America and Australia. Entitled 'Harry Styles Live On Tour' it kicked off with some intimate smaller venues before graduating to massive arenas and was so successful that more dates were added, taking the smash hit tour into 2018.

*He also set records for merchandise sales in more than 50 of the venues.*

'The tour affected me deeply', Harry said. 'It really changed me emotionally having people come to sing the songs. For me the tour was the biggest thing in terms of being more accepting of myself I think. It made me realise people want to see me experiment and have fun. Nobody wants to see you fake it'.

Now Harry was proving he could be a pop superstar in his own right, without the cover and protection of bandmates. He had successfully moved centre stage and was now the front man he was always destined to be.

# Harry's Hits

## The music and acclaim

### The Style Files

*Harry has won .....*

**ARIA Music Awards**
*Harry Styles* album 2017
Best International Artist 2017, 2020, 2022

**Brit Awards**
British Video of the Year 2018 (*Sign of the Times*)
British Single of the Year 2021 (*Watermelon Sugar*)
British Album of the Year 2023 (*Harry's House*)
British Song of the Year 2023 (*As It Was*)
British Artist of the Year 2023
Best Pop/R&B Act 2023

**American Music Awards**
Favourite Pop/Rock album 2020 (*Fine Line*)
Favourite Pop Song 2022 (*As It Was*)
Favourite Male Pop Artist 2022

**Billboard Music Award**
Chart Achievement 2020

**Grammy Award**
Best Pop Solo Performance 2021 (*Watermelon Sugar*)
Album of the Year 2023 (*Harry's House*)
Best Pop Vocal album 2023 (*Harry's House*)

**Juno Awards**
International Album of the Year 2021 (*Fine Line*)
International Album of the Year 2023 (*Harry's House*)

**MTV Video Music Awards**
Best Choreography 2021 (*Treat People with Kindness*)
Best Pop 2023 (*As It Was*)
Best Cinematography 2023 (*As It Was*)
Album of the Year 2023 (*Harry's House*)

*And been nominated for .....*

Two acting ensemble awards (Critic's Choice Movie
Awards and Washington D.C. Area Film Critics
Association Awards (for Dunkirk)

# Harry Styles

## 2017

Harry Styles, his 10-track debut album, was a huge hit — well received by critics and fans alike, selling 230,000 plus copies within the first week of its release in May 2017.

The album was quite a serious work, which music journalists considered fairly derivative of his British rock 1970s musical heroes. In particular the six-minute long single release 'Sign of the Times' was viewed as being heavily influenced by David Bowie.

Harry said that when he came out of the band he didn't want to record 'fun' music; 'I didn't want to make the same music that we were making in the band. Not because I didn't like it ..I just didn't want ..I wanted it to be a different thing.'

Rolling Stone magazine described the release as 'superb ..... (with) an intimately emotional Seventies soft-rock vibe', going on to say that ' ....his sheer brazen confidence is dazzling'.

51

For The Guardian, Alexis Petridis said, 'Styles is remarkably good as a confessional singer-songwriter', while NME's Leonie Cooper said that 'taking inspiration from the best has paid dividends' — a reference to the album's mix of Los Angeles-style classic rock and ballads.

Variety best summed up the album's vibe as being 'a classic cocktail of psychedelia, Britpop and balladry'.

Harry put together a great team to bring the album together, collaborating with Grammy award-winning American record producer and multi-instrumentalist Jeff Bhasker, who has previously worked with Kanye West, Mark Ronson, Alicia Keys and Jay-Z.

The writing team alongside Harry and Jeff comprised Tyler Johnson, Mitch Rowland, Alex Salibian, and Ryan Nasci. All devoted to making the project a success, the team took

Harry Styles AS IT IS

52

THE LATE

# LATE SHOW

[ ] Harry Styles performs during "The Late Late Show with James Corden" — 15 May, 2017

53

themselves off-grid for a two-month stay in Jamaica away from distractions. They threw themselves into their work and reportedly came up with 70-plus possible songs for the album.

As well as all his well-documented musical influences and interests, Harry threw another name into the mix during an interview about the project with USA Today. 'I listened to a lot of Harry Nilsson while making the album,' Harry said. 'His lyrics are honest, and so good, and I think it's because he's never trying to sound clever.'

Describing the album as 'like therapy', Harry continued, 'It's so much easier saying something to an instrument than it is to a person. I kind of decided early on that every time I said to myself, "can I say this?" I wanted to say yes.

'I've never really felt like I've had to explain my personal life and I love that with writing you get to wrap it up with a song. I understand that people will dissect stuff like that, which is amazing, that people care enough about you to try and figure out what it means.'

54

Harry seems to revel in the time and space he is now able to devote to song writing and recording. Back in the 1D days most of the material was written for them and recorded sporadically, often during a day off from touring, in whichever studio was closest and convenient.

The album topped the charts in the US, the UK and Australia and was included in several 'best album' lists that year. Eventually the album went platinum in America and four other countries and overall became the ninth global best-selling album of the year.

Lead single from the album was Sign of the Times — a six-minute long ballad which topped the charts in over 80 countries and made #4 on the Billboard Hot 100. Rolling Stone ranked it as the best song of 2017. Talking to that magazine Harry said, 'Most of the stuff that hurts me about what's going on at the moment is not politics, it's fundamentals. Equal rights. For everyone, all races, sexes, everything.

'Sign of the Times came from "this isn't the first time we've been in a hard time  and it's not going to be the last".  It's written from the point of view as if a mother is told she has five minutes to live after giving birth and has just that short time to tell the child, which is fine,  "Go forth and conquer".'

---

The video for the song was also an attention-grabbing event. Filmed on the Isle of Skye in Scotland, it featured scenes of Harry walking on water and then appearing to levitate and leap off a rock before taking flight and ascending into the clouds.

Harry's first solo tour, in support of his eponymous album, sold close to one million tickets for 89 sell-out shows across Europe, North and South America and Australia. Entitled 'Harry Styles: Live On Tour', it ran from September 2017 to July 2018, kicking off with some intimate smaller venues before graduating to massive arenas and adding dates towards the end.

55

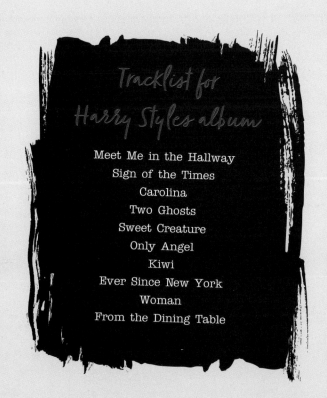

Tracklist for
Harry Styles album

Meet Me in the Hallway
Sign of the Times
Carolina
Two Ghosts
Sweet Creature
Only Angel
Kiwi
Ever Since New York
Woman
From the Dining Table

56

57

[ ] Harry Styles performs onstage at The Greek Theatre in
Los Angeles, California — 20 Sep. 2017

# Fine Line

## 2019

Harry had great plans for his follow up album, Fine Line, feeling determined that it would be a more adventurous work than his debut. 'A lot changes in two years, especially after coming out of the band and just working out what life is now', Harry told US interviewer Howard Stern. 'I feel so much freer, making this album — you get to a place where you feel happy even if the song is about the time when you weren't that happy."

He began work shortly after he had split from his girlfriend Camille Rowe, so he also had a lot of emotional fallout to bring to the project. His producer Kid Harpoon (Tom Hull) encouraged him to use his experiences to help write the songs.

Harry has also said that he took wild mushrooms with hallucinogenic effects as a 'fun creative thing' but added that he'd never do it as an escape from a 'weird place' in his head. He writes most days — not always a whole song, maybe a poem or a line of lyrics — but when working with a team on an album he can devote all his time to the project. Kid Harpoon describes him as 'creative and a hard worker'.

As well as drawing from his usual 70s heroes, other influences on this album include Paul McCartney's Ram album and Joni Mitchell's Blue.

Harry also took more inspiration from his hero David Bowie. Rob Sheffield who joined Harry in the studio to interview him for Rolling Stone magazine, said that Harry kept watching a late-1990s clip of Bowie advising people never to play to the gallery — 'never work for other people in what you do'. Sheffield wrote that this seemed an inspiring pep talk for Harry, '...a reminder not to play it safe. As Bowie says; "If you feel safe in the area that you're working in, you're not working in the right area. Always go a little further into the water than you feel you are capable of being in. Go a little bit out of your depth. And when you don't feel that your feet are quite touching the bottom, you're just about in the right place to do something exciting".'

Tracklist for
Fine Line album

Golden

Watermelon Sugar

Adore You

Lights Up

Cherry

Falling

To Be So Lonely

She

Sunflower, Vol. 6

Canyon Moon

Treat People With Kindness

Fine Line

60

[ ] Harry Styles attends a Spotify private listening
session for fans in LA — 11 December, 2019

As with his first album, Harry worked with a team of his favourite collaborators, Tyler Johnson, Mitch Rowland, Sammy Witte, Jeff Bhasker, Greg Kurstin and Amy Allen. 'If you're going in with session writers or something, you spend one or two days there, and there is no way that person really cares about your album as much as you do', Harry told Rolling Stone magazine. 'I know that Mitch, Tyler, Tom, Sammy, and Jeff wanted the album to be as good as I wanted to be. They don't care if it's their song or not. They're not concerned how many songs they get on an album. They want it to be the best album it can possibly be.'

Work on the album was split between Nashville, LA, and the Shangri-La studios in Malibu, California – and the overall sound is very Californian. It was recorded in Wiltshire, UK, at the Real World studio owned by Peter Gabriel.

Instrumentally it uses strings, including a double bass, horns, even a gospel choir on Treat People with Kindness. Harry's team also tracked down the woman who built dulcimers for Joni Mitchell and these were used throughout the album. They are a type of soundbox, similar to a zither, and their sound is dotted throughout the album.

In October 2019 the first single from the album was released, Lights Up, which reached #3 on the British charts. The second single release was Adore You which reached #6 on the Billboard chart.

Then the album came out on 13 December 2019 and subsequently spawned another four hit singles; Falling, Watermelon Sugar, Golden, and Treat People with Kindness.

Fine Line made its debut at #3 in the UK and #1 in the US, giving Harry his second consecutive number-one album in America, where it has since gone double platinum.

Harry told Rolling Stone that the album was 'all about having sex and feeling sad'. The dedication on the album reads; 'To all that I've done, the good and the bad. That is life'.

Critics found a lot of good in the album. For NME, Hannah Mylrea said the album 'had far more of a cohesive Styles sound' and, lyrically, was 'brazenly honest'. She gave it four stars, concluding; 'It's an elegant combination of the ex-boy-bander's influences, slick modern pop and his own roguish charm.'

Rolling Stone's Nick Catucci found the album to be 'Retro-rock with a sensitive touch …. a streamlined, party-ready, primary colours take on the enduring concept of the rock & roll star man…. It's also as much fun as anyone short of Bruno Mars is having with a band these days.'

## 'Dextrous and audacious' declared Alexandra Pollard of the UK's Independent newspaper.

The album won an American Music Award (Favourite Pop/Rock album) and an ARIA music award (Best International Artist) and was nominated for Brit and Grammy awards.

63

## Watermelon Sugar

Watermelon Sugar was a huge hit from this album – the sound of summer 2020. It was first released in November 2019 as a promotional single, then had a full release the following year when it took off like a rocket. It gave Harry his first solo #1 on the Billboard Hot 100 chart and his first Grammy win, picking up the prize for Best Pop Solo Performance going platinum by October 2020. Despite his early massive success with One Direction, a Grammy win had eluded him until now. So this award was incredibly special. The accompanying music video, showing Harry picnicking on a beach, had received over 332.6 million views on YouTube by May 2020.

65

[ ] Harry Styles performs on stage during Radio 1's Big
Weekend 2022 in Coventry, England — 29 May, 2022

# Harry's House

## 2022

A lot happened after the release of Fine Line. Forced to cancel the planned tour around the album because of the Covid 19 pandemic lockdowns, Harry bubbled up with friends at his home in Los Angeles. Like everyone else they kept busy - walking and cooking were popular pastimes - but also for almost the first time since stepping on the celebrity merry go round as a 16 year old X Factor contestant, Harry had some time off and an opportunity to think - something he hadn't really had time to do since finding fame aged 16 after X Factor. It was time well spent, as he told Spout podcast 'I used to be so afraid of who I was if I didn't do it [music] and I don't feel afraid of that anymore and I think in a lot of ways that allows me to just enjoy it more. I've always felt incredibly lucky to get to do this as my job, and more and more I feel incredibly lucky that this is what I get to do, and I feel like I'm falling more and more in love with making music each time I get to do it.'

66

Given the circumstances of the pandemic and the enforced separations it required, it's probably not surprising that he also thought about the idea of home. 'I realised that that home feeling isn't something that you get from a house; it's more of an internal thing,' he said in an April 2022 interview with Better Homes and Gardens. 'You realise that when you stop for a minute,'

A few months later he began writing for his next album and when Rick Rubin's Shangri-La studio in Malibu became available, Harry started recording with long time collaborators Kid Harpoon and Tyler Johnson. Taking inspiration from influential Japanese musician Haruomi Hosono's 1973 album Hosono House, Harry pursued the idea of producing a series of songs to act as an internal monologue, as if journaling a day in his life. The 13-track album finally produced, flecked with influences from the 1970s and 80s artists Harry so admires, includes the most intimate recordings of his career so far.

## Tracklist for Harry's House

Music For a Sushi Restaurant

Late Night Talking

Grapejuice

As It Was

Daylight

Little Freak

Matilda

Cinema

Daydreaming

Keep Driving

Satellite

Boyfriends

Love of My Life

(Harry has said that Harry's House is the album he has always wanted to make and which feels the most like him, naming Matilda and Little Freak as his personal favourite tracks.)

68

69

Seeking to create music that was very different to Fine Line, Harry told Better Homes and Gardens June 2022 edition that he had been extremely careful about what he listened to while writing for this third album – choosing mostly classical works and arrangements – because he wanted a reset of his previous sonic references in order to begin writing music afresh with 'a blank canvas'.

'I think everyone went through a big moment of self-reflection, a lot of navel-gazing, and I don't know if there's anything more navel-gazing than making an album. It's so self-absorbed," he said.

But however personal it seemed to Harry, the themes and reference he chose for the album chimed with listeners who lapped it all up. Following its release on 20 May 2022 the album became the fastest-selling record of the year on both sides of the Atlantic and reached number one in 27 countries around the world. Along the way it gained multi-platinum certifications and sold more than 330,000 units worldwide.

Critics generally loved the album as much as fans, with NME reviewer Rhian Daly in the UK saying it would solidify Harry 'as one of the current pop landscapes' greats', while The Guardian newspaper thought it had 'abundant charm' [making it] 'a perfect reflection of the pop star who made it'.

Across the Atlantic, The New York Times said Harry's House was, 'the most distinct-sounding album Styles has made yet, and his production team of Kid Harpoon and Tyler Johnson ..... concoct some vivid sonic landscapes' while describing Harry's vocals as 'sleek and nimble throughout, favoring a looser delivery — he actually scats on one song — than the flashy, belt-it-out pyrotechnics of his boy band days'.

Rolling Stone magazine said the album was 'a smooth, sensitive step forward for one of pop's most likeable stars', concluding that 'he's pulled off the neat trick of making his music at once elegant and refined but also warmer and more intimate. Harry's

House is bright with synths and horns, often steeped in slick, sticky synth-pop and R&B...This is a Santa Ana summer breeze of a record.'

Pitchfork thought Harry wore 'his influences more lightly' on this album, saying; 'Its sounds—which move through funk, folk, and 2010s Tumblr-pop—are friendly and familiar enough to satisfy passive listening, but deftly executed, with a surplus of style and whimsy that rewards a more active ear'.

Plaudits from the music industry followed. Never mind Harry's 'house', the stages of the 2023 award ceremonies effectively became Harry's home, so much time did he spend accepting awards.

In the UK, having ended 2022 as the best-selling artist on both the album and the singles charts – for Harry's House and As It Was respectively – Harry enjoyed a memorable night at the Brit Awards in February 2023 where he led the field with four nominations. He won them all – best British Album of the Year (Harry's House) Best British Song of the Year (As It Was) British Artist of the Year 2023 and Best Pop/R&B Act.

While accepting his second award of the evening Harry thanked his mum for secretly entering him for X Factor, then thrilled fans by namechecking every member of One Direction 'Niall, Liam, Louis and Zayn, because I wouldn't be here without you either,' he said. 'Thank you so much.'

71

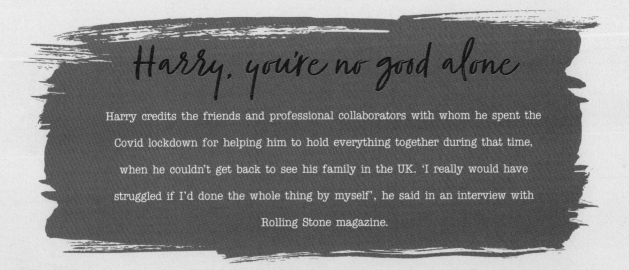

## Harry, you're no good alone

Harry credits the friends and professional collaborators with whom he spent the Covid lockdown for helping him to hold everything together during that time, when he couldn't get back to see his family in the UK. 'I really would have struggled if I'd done the whole thing by myself', he said in an interview with Rolling Stone magazine.

72

[ ] Harry Styles performs on the Coachella stage during the Coachella
Valley Music And Arts Festival, Indio, California — 22 April, 2022

Harry also told Better Homes and Gardens that he'd enjoyed making Harry's House because, 'Finally, it doesn't feel like my life is over if this album isn't a commercial success.' He went on to explain that was because when he first left One Direction he didn't feel he could make 'fun' music if he wanted to be taken seriously as a musician. Then, while he felt 'freer' with Fine Line, it's only now that 'I just want to make stuff

# As It Was

As It Was has become Harry's biggest song yet – which is saying something. It got to #1 in more than two dozen countries, including 10 weeks in America. In the UK the track had the additional kudos of being the only one to surpass 180 million streams during 2022, according to analysis of Official Charts data by the British Phonographic Industry (BPI)

The 1980s-inspired lead single on Harry's House, about 'embracing change, losing oneself, finding oneself'- was released on 1 April 2022.

74

Fans snapped up the track to give Harry his second #1 after Sign of the Times five years before. The song spent 10 weeks at the top of the UK Singles Chart, becoming the best-selling and longest running #1 of the year. It also gave Harry his second #1 in America, (the first being Watermelon Sugar) and spent 15 weeks at the top of the Billboard 100 which made the track the longest running #1 by any UK act and the fourth longest in the chart's history. On top of this success on both sides of the Atlantic, the track went to #1 in 45 countries including Australia and most of Europe.

In the UK, NME and The Guardian both rated the track five out of five stars while in the US, Rolling Stone's review praised the track as one of Harry's most 'emotionally powerful', describing it as a 'straight-from-the-heart cry that's also an irresistible dance-floor challenge'.

The track opens with a line spoken by Harry's goddaughter Ruby Winston (daughter of his old friend Ben Winston from One Direction days) who says 'Come on, Harry, we want to say goodnight to you'.

that is right, that is fun, in terms of the process, that I can be proud of for a long time, that my friends can be proud of, that my family can be proud of, that my kids will be proud of one day," he said.

Well everyone family, friends and fans alike were very proud when the following year Harry went on to cement his status as one of the biggest pop stars on the planet by picking up the prestigious and hotly contested Grammy award for Album of the Year. Beating off tough competition from Adele, Abba, Bad Bunny, Beyonce, Brandi Carlile, Mary J. Blige, Coldplay, Kendrick Lamar, and Lizzo, Harry began his acceptance speech by acknowledging the array of talent he'd been up against. 'I've been so, so inspired by every artist in this category with me at a lot of different times in my life, I've listened to everyone in this category, when I'm alone " Harry said. ' And I think – like on nights like tonight – it's obviously so important for us to remember that there is no such thing as best in music'.

Having been nominated for six awards that night, bringing his total number of Grammy nominations as a solo artist to nine, Harry added to his tally for the evening by also winning the Best Pop Vocal Album prize. He also got to perform on the Grammy stage, singing his #1 hit single As It Was, which was among the nominations for Song of the Year and Record of the Year. Harry wore a pale silver sequinned and fringed catsuit as he led his back up dancers in recreating the aesthetic of the original music video which included a moving walkway.

75

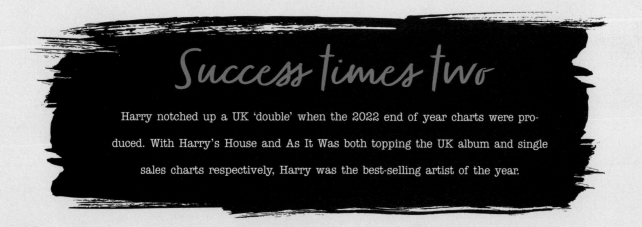

## Success times two

Harry notched up a UK 'double' when the 2022 end of year charts were produced. With Harry's House and As It Was both topping the UK album and single sales charts respectively, Harry was the best-selling artist of the year.

76

77

# Harry's Homies
## Musical collaborators and influences

## Kid Harpoon

Kid Harpoon is the stage name of British singer-songwriter and producer Tom Hull, and a key member of the team around Harry, most often as a producer and co-writer.

Born on 20 April 1982, Kid started playing guitar when he was 12 and began writing songs soon after. He was influenced by a wide range of music genres, including folk, punk, and indie rock. He began performing live in the mid-2000s, gaining attention for his distinctive voice and emotionally charged lyrics. In 2007, he released his debut EP, called The First EP, which received critical acclaim and led to a recording contract with influential indie label Young Turks.

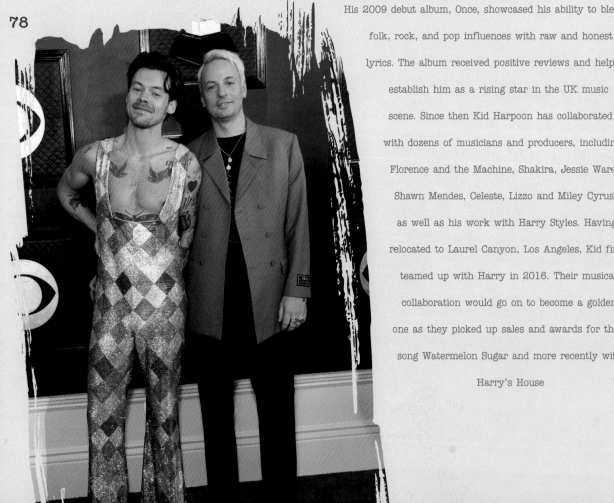

His 2009 debut album, Once, showcased his ability to blend folk, rock, and pop influences with raw and honest lyrics. The album received positive reviews and helped establish him as a rising star in the UK music scene. Since then Kid Harpoon has collaborated with dozens of musicians and producers, including Florence and the Machine, Shakira, Jessie Ware, Shawn Mendes, Celeste, Lizzo and Miley Cyrus, as well as his work with Harry Styles. Having relocated to Laurel Canyon, Los Angeles, Kid first teamed up with Harry in 2016. Their musical collaboration would go on to become a golden one as they picked up sales and awards for their song Watermelon Sugar and more recently with Harry's House

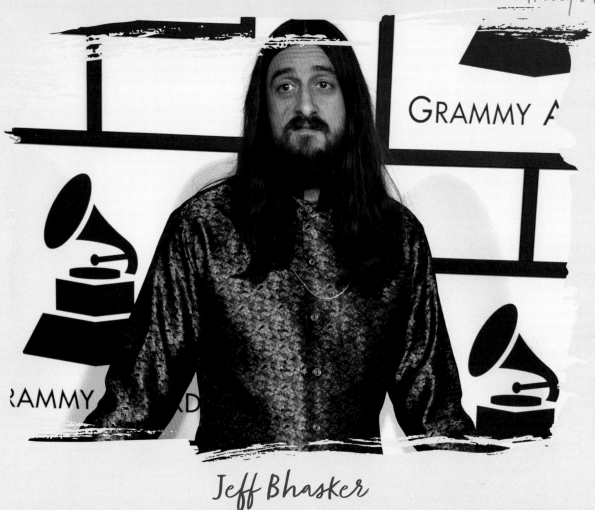

# Jeff Bhasker

Jeff Bhasker is an American record producer, songwriter, and multi-instrumentalist who has worked with the biggest names in the music business. He was born 4 March 1974 in Kansas, to an American mother and an Indian father, and grew up in New Mexico. After studying jazz piano and arranging at Berklee College of Music in Boston, Massachusetts, he played with the 1970s-era R&B band Tavares, before moving to New York in 2001. He rose to prominence in the mid-2000s, producing hits for artists such as Jay-Z, Kanye West, and Alicia Keys.

His time as a producer and co-writer with Harry began in 2017 when he was hired to work on his solo debut album. Since then, he has become a key collaborator on Harry's music, contributing to hit songs such as Sign of the Times and Adore You. As a producer, Jeff is known for his ability to blend different musical genres, creating a sound that is both unique and commercially successful. In addition to his work with Harry Styles, Bhasker has produced music for a range of artists, including Bruno Mars, Kanye West, and Beyonce.

Harry Styles performs on the Coachella stage during the Coachella Valley
Music And Arts Festival, Indio, California — 22 April, 2022

# Tyler Johnson

American singer songwriter, producer and multi-instrumentalist – and frequent collaborator with Jeff Bhasker - Tyler Johnson has worked with Harry on all three of his albums. Born 26 November 1986, he grew up in a musical family in Orlando, Florida, where his mother was a gospel singer, and his father was a jazz pianist, which combined to inspire him to pursue music at a young age. Having started playing the piano at the age of four, Tyler began writing songs as a teenager and then attended Berklee College of Music in Boston, where he honed his skills as a songwriter and producer.

After graduating, Tyler moved to Los Angeles to pursue a career in the music industry. He worked as an assistant engineer at a recording studio and spent his free time writing and producing music. In 2010, he signed a publishing deal and has since gone on to write and produce music for some of the biggest names in the music industry, including as well as Harry, Ed Sheeran, and Camila Cabello.

82

# Mitch Rowland

Mitch Rowland is an American musician, guitarist, singer, and songwriter, born 1 October 1988, in Tulsa, Oklahoma. He moved to Los Angeles in 2013 and started playing in local bars and clubs which is where he caught the attention of Harry, who was looking for a guitarist for his solo tour.

Mitch joined Harry Styles' band in 2017 and has since become an integral part of his live performances and studio recordings. He has co-written several songs with Harry, including Carolina, Kiwi, and Ever Since New York. Mitch's soulful guitar playing has been a highlight of Styles' performances, and he has been praised for his ability to bring a unique sound to Harry's music.

# Alex Salibian

Part of Jeff Bhasker's production crew, Alex Salibian is an American musician, songwriter, and record producer known for his work with Camila Cabello, Kendrick Lamar, and John Legend, as well as Harry Styles. He was born on 22 August 1985 in Chicago, Illinois, and began playing the guitar at the age of 11.

Admired for his attention to detail and ability to blend genres seamlessly, Alex is also a versatile musician, playing multiple instruments on many of the songs he produces, which have included Harry's first hit single as a solo artist, Sign of the Times. In addition to his work in the studio, Salibian has also released music as a solo artist. His debut EP, All Things Real, was released in 2018 and showcased a unique blend of folk, rock, and pop music.

# Greg Kurstin

Greg Kurstin is a Grammy award-winning American record producer, songwriter, and musician whose career began in the 1990s. He was born on 14 May 1969, in Los Angeles, California, and later studied jazz piano at The New School in New York City. After playing with various bands and collaborating with artists such as Beck and The Flaming Lips, Greg shifted his focus to producing and song writing, in the early 2000s and quickly made a name for himself in the industry. He has produced and co-written some of the biggest hits of the past decade, including Adele's Hello, Sia's Chandelier, and Pink's What About Us.

He co-wrote and produced the majority of the songs on Harry Styles' self-titled debut album, and the pair continued their collaboration on Fine Line where Greg co-wrote and produced several of the album's tracks, including the hit singles Adore You and Watermelon Sugar.

# Ryan Nasci

New Yorker Ryan Nasci is another member of the small team Jeff Bhasker put around Harry to work on his first album. He's a songwriter, guitarist and studio engineer known for his soulful sound and emotive lyrics.

# Sammy Witte

Since joining Harry's first solo tour in 2017, American musician and producer Sam Witte has played a key role in Harry's career. As well as working as a producer and musical director for Harry, Sam has contributed to his studio recordings and helped shape the sound of hit singles such as Adore You and Watermelon Sugar, and the album Fine Line.

# Amy Allen

American singer-songwriter Amy Allen who has made a name for herself in the music industry as a prolific songwriter. Born on 13 October 1993, in Los Angeles, California, she later honed her skills at Berklee College of Music, where she graduated with a degree in song writing. Her big break came in 2018 when she co-wrote Back to You for Selena Gomez and he shas since written hit songs for several other artists, including Halsey, and Dua Lipa, as well as Harry Styles for whom she co-wrote Adore You.

She's been praised for her unique melodies and catchy hooks, as well as her ability to capture raw emotions and personal experiences in her lyrics which often touch on themes of love, heartbreak, and self-discovery. In addition to her work as a songwriter, Allen has released music as a solo artist. Her debut EP, "Get Me Outta Here!", was released in 2019.

85

[ ] Harry Styles attends the "My Policeman" Premiere during the Toronto
International Film Festival, Toronto, Ontario — 11 Sep. 2022

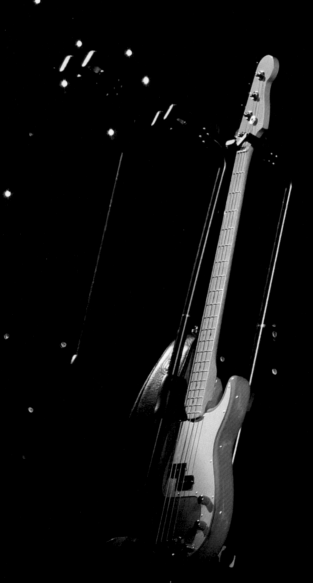

87

# Lights Up

## Harry on Tour

Harry's live concert performances win him almost universal praise — he's a natural performer with stage presence and charm, fortified with impressive vocals and, of course, incredible material.

⌐⌐ Harry Styles performs at Radio City Music Hall.
NYC — 28 September 28, 2017

# Harry Styles: Live on Tour

Fans were at fever pitch for Harry's first tour which kicked off on 19 September 2017 in San Francisco. According to Variety he sold just under one million tickets for 89 shows throughout the UK, Europe, America, Asia and Australia.

The 10-month long tour included many firsts for Harry — not least of which was to prove that he could carry a show as a solo performer. His performances were widely acclaimed, leaving no one in any doubt of his talent and star quality. The tour began in small venues, before graduating to massive arenas. He commanded some stellar opening acts too, including country music star Kacey Musgraves and soul star Leon Bridges.

Along the way he created so many sweet, crowd-pleasing moments for his fans, including helping a woman to come out as bi-sexual to her parents in San Jose. He spotted and read out to the crowd a sign being held aloft by the fan called Grace which said; 'I'm gonna come out to my parents because of you!!!' He then asked the audience at the SAP Centre to quieten down while he spoke to Grace and found out her mother's name was Tina, before going on to shout into his microphone, supposedly to her mother who was in a hotel four miles away; 'Tina, she's gay!' He then pretended to hear the response, 'Tina says she loves ya. Congratulations I'm very happy for you.'

# Harry Styles: Live on Tour dates

## 2017

19 September, Masonic Auditorium, San Francisco, USA

20 September, Greek Theatre, Los Angeles, USA

25 September, Ryman Auditorium, Nashville, USA

26 September, Chicago Theatre, Chicago, USA

28 September, Radio City Music Hall, New York, USA

30 September, Wang Theatre, Boston, USA


1 October, Dar Constitution Hall, Washington D.C.,USA

4 October, Massey Hall, Toronto, Canada

5 October, Tower Theatre, Upper Darby, USA

8 October, Coca Cola Roxy Theatre, Atlanta, USA

10 October, The Pavilion, Irving, USA

11 October, Moody Theatre, Austin, USA

14 October, Comerica Theatre, Phoenix, USA

25 October, Olympia, Paris, France

27 October, Palladium, Cologne, Germany,

29,30 October, Eventim Apollo, London, England


1 November, O2 Apollo, Manchester, England

2 November, SEC Armadillo, Glasgow, Scotland

5 November, Fryshuset, Stockholm, Sweden

7 November, Tempodrom, Berlin, Germany

8 November, AFAS Live, Amsterdam, Netherlands

10 November, Discoteca Alcatraz, Milan, Italy

19 November, Mercedes Benz Arena, Shanghai, China

23 November, The Star Centre, Singapore

26 November, Enmore Theatre, Sydney, Australia

30 November, Forum Theatre, Melbourne, Australia


2 December, Spark Arena, Auckland, New Zealand

7,8 December, Ex Theatre Roppongi, Tokyo, Japan

Grace filmed the whole thing and showed her mother reporting back on Twitter afterwards that Tina was overjoyed and replied, 'Yes I do love you and you can be whoever you want to be.'

Harry also serenaded a couple expecting a baby in Detroit and regularly waved flags for Pride and Black Lives Matter.

He continually demonstrated his support for the idea that everyone is entitled to be whoever they want to be. Many of his concerts opened with Harry telling the arena; 'be whoever it is you want to be in this room tonight'.

As well as all that, Harry did his bit to save the planet by encouraging water conservation. Working with the Reverb organisation, the tour made a big effort with recycling, saving the equivalent of 10,000 single use water bottles by fans and 3,200 from Harry's band and crew, as well as recycling thousands of gallons of water backstage.

He also promoted the work of the US charity HeadCount as they registered hundreds of his young fans at his concerts to sign up as voters.

His shows themselves were widely acclaimed. The Los Angeles Times described his appearance in LA as being 'one of the best arena shows of the last few years', going on to rate the stage production as 'classy and minimal, relying on the strength of the songs and [Harry's] charm as a live performer.'

Billboard said Harry was 'a true rock star', while The Independent newspaper in the UK said that 'Most performers can only dream of having the charisma and star quality that Harry Styles naturally exudes'.

New York style magazine The Cut decided that Harry was 'the perfect

Harry Styles performs at Radio City Music Hall, NYC — 28 September 28, 2017

## 2018

11 March, St. Jakobshalle, Basel, Switzerland

13 March, AccorHotels Arena, Paris, France

14 March, Ziggo Dome, Amsterdam, Netherlands

16 March, Sportpaleis, Antwerp, Belgium

18 March, Ericsson Globe, Stockholm, Sweden

19 March, Royal Arena, Copenhagen, Denmark

21 March, Oslo Spektrum, Oslo, Norway

24 March, König Pilsener Arena, Oberhausen, Germany

25 March, Barclays Arena, Hamburg, Germany

27 March, Olympiahalle, Munich, Germany

30 March, Palau Sant Jordi, Barcelona, Spain

31 March, WiZink Center, Madrid, Spain

2 April, Mediolanum Forum, Milan, Italy

4 April, Unipol Arena, Bologna, Italy

5 April, SAP Arena, Mannheim, Germany

7 April, Genting Arena, Birmingham, England

9 April, Manchester Arena, Manchester, England

11,12 April, O2 Arena, London, England

14 April, SSE Hydro, Glasgow, Scotland

16 April, 3 Arena, Dublin, Ireland

21 April, Perth Arena, Perth, Australia

24 April, Hisense Arena, Melbourne, Australia

27 April, Qudos Bank Arena, Sydney, Australia

28 April, Brisbane Entertainment Centre, Brisbane, Australia

1 May, Mall of Asia Arena, Manila, Philippines

3 May, Singapore Indoor Stadium, Singapore

5 May, HKCEC Hall 5BC, Hong Kong

7 May, Impact Arena, Bangkok, Thailand

10 May, World Memorial Hall, Osaka, Japan

12 May, Makuhari Event Hall, Chiba, Japan

23 May, DirecTV Arena, Buenos Aires, Argentina

25 May, Movistar Arena, Santiago, Chile

27 May, Jeunesse Arena, Rio de Janeiro, Brazil

29 May, Espaco das Americas, Sao Paulo, Brazil


1,2 June, Palacio de los Deportes, Mexico City, Mexico

5 June, American Airlines Centre, Dallas, USA

7 June, Toyota Centre, Houston, USA

9 June, BB&T Centre, Sunrise, USA

11 June, Infinite Energy Arena, Duluth, USA

12 June, Bridgestone Arena, Nashville, USA

14 June, Hersheypark Stadium, Hershey, USA

15 June, Wells Fargo Centre, Philadelphia, USA

16 June, Air Canada Centre, Toronto, Canada

18 June, TD Garden, Boston, USA

21,22 June, Madison Square Garden, New York, USA

24 June, Capital One Arena, Washington D.C., USA

26 June, Little Caesars Arena, Detroit, USA

27 June, Bankers Life Fieldhouse, Indianapolis, USA

30 June, United Centre, Chicago, USA


1 July, Xcel Energy Centre, St Paul, USA

3 July, Pepsi Centre, Denver, USA

6 July, Rogers Arena, Vancouver, Canada

7 July, Key Arena, Seattle, USA

9 July, Golden 1 Centre, Sacramento, USA

11 July, SAP Centre, San Jose, USA

13/14 July, The Forum, Inglewood, USA

93

[ ] Harry Styles performs onstage during Harry Styles: Live
On Tour — Madison Square Garden, NYC— 21 June, 2018

Harry Styles performs onstage during Harry Styles: Live On Tour
— Madison Square Garden, NYC — 21 June, 2018

95

## Live On Tour support acts

### 2017

**Muna (USA and Europe)**
An American rock/electro pop band consisting
of Katie Gavin, Josette Maskin, and Naomi
McPherson

**Maddy Jane (Australia)**
Australian singer/songwriter and guitarist with
an indie/punk rock vibe

**Mabel (UK and Europe)**
Brit award-winning British singer/songwriter of
'Don't Call Me Up' fame

### 2018

**The Preatures (Australia)**
Rock/pop/soul band from Sydney

**Warpaint (Asia)**
Four-piece American indie/rock band from
California

**Leon Bridges (Latin America)**
American soul singer and songwriter
Kacey Musgraves (US and Canada)
Multi Grammy and Country Music award-winning
American singer songwriter

96

crush. Slinking around [the stage] in the drama of big pants and a Mick Jagger femme

blouse he looks like a rascal androgyne, he acts like a romantic, he's all chin scruff and

non-threatening sex appeal'.

For their part his audiences are more respectful of his music than was the case with One

Direction when audience noise could often drown out the sound — but there is still quite

a lot of screaming and singing along. His fans have grown up with him and are now

typically mid-20s, rather than teenagers. They usually strip the merchandise stand of its

[ ] Harry Styles performs a live concert at Royal Arena,
Copenhagen — March, 2018

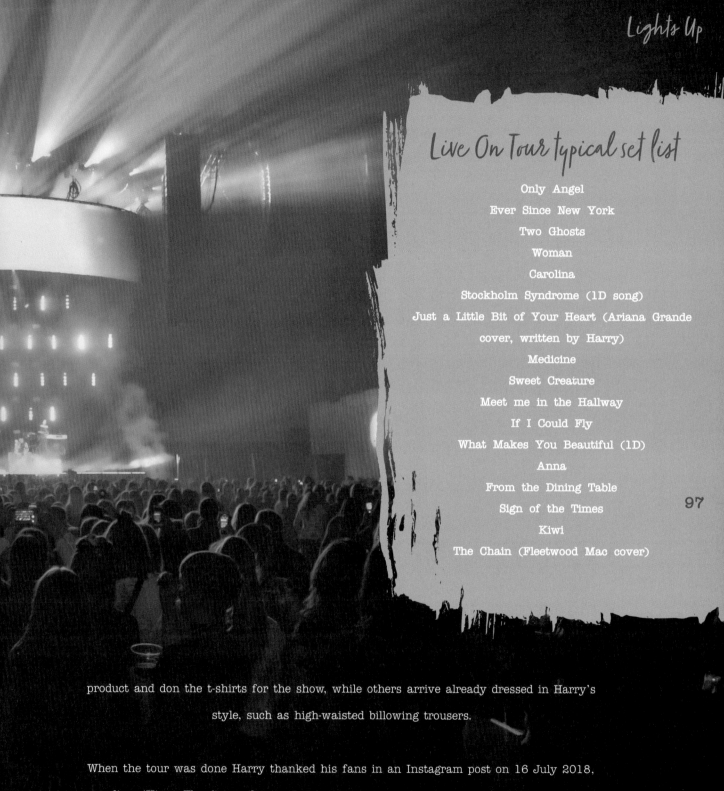

## Live On Tour typical set list

Only Angel

Ever Since New York

Two Ghosts

Woman

Carolina

Stockholm Syndrome (1D song)

Just a Little Bit of Your Heart (Ariana Grande
cover, written by Harry)

Medicine

Sweet Creature

Meet me in the Hallway

If I Could Fly

What Makes You Beautiful (1D)

Anna

From the Dining Table

Sign of the Times

Kiwi

The Chain (Fleetwood Mac cover)

product and don the t-shirts for the show, while others arrive already dressed in Harry's
style, such as high-waisted billowing trousers.

When the tour was done Harry thanked his fans in an Instagram post on 16 July 2018,
reading; 'Kissy. Thank you for coming out to see us, it has been a pleasure playing for
you all. I'm off to write some more music and I hope I'll be seeing you again very soon.
Thank you to my band, the crew, and all of you for making his tour so wonderful. Treat

98

[ ] Harry Styles performs for SiriusXM and Pandora in New York City at Music Hall of Williamsburg — 28 February, 2020

99

Lights Up

# Harry Styles: Love On Tour

Harry's second world tour has been a triumph. Wherever he plays, the venue becomes 'Harry's House' - a space filled with love and acceptance. As he dances around the stage with props thrown to him by fans - everything from stuffed toys to balloons and feather boas - his joy is infectious and everyone is happy in Harry's candy-coloured, accepting world. For the two plus hours Harry and his fans are together, everything is good and love is in the air. People are treated with kindness and feel safe.

He maintained his tradition of really interacting with fans, who communicate with him by waving signs. He'll often take a sign or begin a conversation about what someone has written. Appearing in Germany on the day abortion laws changed in America, Harry grabbed a sign saying 'My Body, My Choice' and showed it to the whole audience.

But serious moments like that are interspersed with the type of fun and cheeky asides which so endear Harry to his audiences. Joking over splitting his trousers, inciting ecstatic screams with his dance moves and high kicks, Harry has a plethora of stage antics to entertain the crowd.

Stage design is relatively low-key compared to some other stars selling out stadiums - pyrotechnics and elaborate set pieces are not Harry's style.
However on stage he does elevate his fashion even further. He is simply knock out. Whether he's in a candy cane-striped sparkling catsuit or a shirtless suit, Harry's costumes are as playful as his performances.

# On the road

Harry runs a tight ship while touring. It's reported that his routine while on the road includes:

➤ 10 hours sleep each night

➤ IV injections of vitamins and other nutrients

➤ Strict diet excluding coffee, alcohol and other foods that could affect singing voice

➤ Humidifiers in his bedroom to stop the air getting too dry and affecting his throat

101

[ ] Harry Styles performs onstage during the tour opener for Love On Tour, Las Vegas — 4 Sep. 2021

Songs from Harry's House dominate the setlist but of course, he still performs many of the most popular songs from previous albums including Golden and Adore you from Fine Line, as well as Sign of the Times from his debut. He also includes his version of What Makes You Beautiful, an iconic song from his former band One Direction.

Originally planned to begin in Spring 2020 in support of his Fine Line album, the tour was twice postponed because of the worldwide Covid 19 pandemic and eventually got going in America on 4 September 2021 in Las Vegas. After completing 42 dates in the States, Harry then set off on a world tour promoting his third album Harry's House as well. With extra dates added along the way, the tour eventually consisted of seven legs over 22 months, ending in Italy in July 2023.

It was a staggering undertaking. The itinerary was mind-boggling, including huge venues and stadiums across every continent.

His sell-out shows included an impressive 15-night residency at New York's Madison Square Garden in August 2022, which The New York Times described as, 'an impressive feat befitting one of the most popular musicians in the world'. In a five star review of Harry's Wembley Stadium concert on 18 June 2022, NME described his concert as 'a powerful, inclusive and celebratory pop carnival' in which he 'cranks the showmanship up to 11 as he proves more than capable of electrifying a vast venue'.

## Coachella – 15 April 2022

Harry Styles surprised his audience at Coachella with a special guest appearance by Shania Twain. To strains of her 1997 hit 'Man, I Feel Like a Woman', country music star Shania rose on a platform from behind the stage, in a sequinned dress to match Harry's lowcut jumpsuit, and the couple finished her iconic song together. Harry has often referenced Shania as being one of his big musical influences and he took the opportunity to thank her again in person at Coachella, telling the audience, 'In the car, with my mother, as a child this lady taught me to sing' .

[ ] Harry Styles performs on the
Coachella stage with Shania Twain
during the Coachella Valley Music
And Arts Festival, Indio, California —
22 April, 2022

# Love On Tour support acts

## 2021

### Jenny Lewis
American singer/songwriter and actress, best known as former front woman for indie rock band Rilo Kiley

### Madison Cunningham
American West Coast folk-rocker, whose Americana album Who Are You Now is among Harry's favourites

### Orville Peck
South African country musician who wears a fringed mask to cover his face

## 2022

### Mitski
Japanese/American indie rock singer/songwriter famous for her pithy yet intense songs

### Arlo Parks
British singer-songwriter and poet whose breakthrough came with her debut single Cola in 2018

### Wolf Alice
English rock band and winners of 2022 Brit Award for British Group of the Year

### Madi Diaz
American singer-songwriter known for her indie pop sound and themes of relationships and identity.

### Blood Orange
Blood Orange is a musical project by British artist Dev Hynes, known for its blend of funk, R&B, and indie pop.

### Gabriels
Soulful American trio led by Jacob Lusk whose roots are in spiritual music

### Jessie Ware
English singer songwriter whose music is a blend of R&B, hip-hop, pop and soul

### Ben Harper
American singer songwriter, guitarist and multi-instrumentalist whose sound mixes blues, folk, soul, reggae, and rock

**Koffee**
This Jamaican singer, rapper, DJ, and guitarist, real name Mikayla Simpson, specialises in a vibrant mix of dancehall, contemporary reggae, and rap

**DJ Kamilla Rose**
Canadian DJ and producer known for her eclectic mixes of hip-hop, R&B, and electronic music

**Wet Leg**
Punk-inspired British Indie rock group

**Ny Oh**
New Zealand-based musician with an indie-folk/pop sound

**Inhaler**
Energetic Irish rock band fronted by singer Eli Hewson, son of U2's Bono

NB - Asia to be announced

From acting as a quasi-ringmaster for everything from marriage proposals to baby gender reveals, Harry continued to get up close and personal with the fans at his shows. There were also a few other surprises, including at a Sydney, Australia show in March 2023 when Harry was joined on stage by legendary Australian singer Daryl Braithwaite. Harry has performed Daryl's 1990s hit Horses at his Australian gigs for several years. The song has become a modern Australian classic and the crowd went wild as Daryl himself walked onto the stage to duet with Harry during his 4 March show at the Accor Stadium.

## 2021

4 September, MGM Grand Garden Arena, Las Vegas, USA

7 September, Ball Arena, Denver, USA

9 September, AT&T Center, San Antonio, USA

11 September, American Airlines Center, Dallas, USA

15 September, Enterprise Center, St Louis, USA

17 September, Wells Fargo Center, Philadelphia, USA

18 September, Capital One Arena, Washington D.C., USA

20 September, Little Caesars Arena, Detroit, USA

22 September, Xcel Energy Center, Saint Paul, USA

24/25 September, United Center, Chicago, USA

29 September, Bridgestone Arena, Nashville, USA


1 October, Bridgestone Arena, Nashville, USA

3/4 October, Madison Square Garden, New York City, USA

7 October, Amway Center, Orlando, USA

8 October, FLA Live Arena, Sunrise, USA

10 October, Amalie Arena, Tampa, USA

12 October, PNC Arena, Raleigh, USA

14 October, PPG Paints Arena, Pittsburgh, USA

16 October, Madison Square Garden, New York City, USA

18 October, Rocket Mortgage FieldHouse, Cleveland, USA

21/23 October, Mohegan Sun Arena, Uncasville, USA

25 October, TD Garden, Boston, USA

27/28 October, State Farm Arena, Atlanta, USA

30/31 October, Madison Square Garden, New York City, USA


1 November, Fiserv Forum, Milwaukee, USA

7 November, Tacoma Dome, Tacoma, USA

8 November, Moda Center, Portland, USA

10 November, Golden 1 Center, Sacramento, USA

11 November, SAP Center, San Jose, USA

13 November, Gila River Arena, Glendale, USA

15 November, Pechanga Arena, San Diego, USA

17/19/20 November, The Forum, Inglewood, USA

23 November, Toyota Center, Houston, USA

24 November, Simmons Bank Arena, North Little Rock, USA

28 November, UBS Arena, Elmont, USA

107

Harry Styles performs onstage during the tour opener for Love On Tour, Las Vegas — 4 Sep, 2021

2022

11 June, Ibrox Stadium, Glasgow, Scotland

15/16 June, Emirates Old Trafford, Manchester, England

18/19 June, Wembley Stadium, London, England

22 June, Aviva Stadium, Dublin, Ireland

26 June, Volksparkstadion, Hamburg, Germany

29 June, Tele2 Arena, Stockholm, Sweden


1 July, Telenor Arena, Oslo, Norway

5 July, Accor Arena, Paris, France

7 July, Sportpaleis, Antwerp, Belgium

9 July, ZiggoDome, Amsterdam, Netherlands

11 July, Olympiahalle, Munich, Germany

13 July, Budapest Sports Arena, Budapest, Hungary

15 July, O2 Arena, Prague, Czech Republic

16 July, Weiner Stadthalle, Vienna, Austria

18 July, Tauron Arena, Krakow, Poland

20 July, Mercedes-Benz Arena, Berlin, Germany

22 July, Lanxess Arena, Cologne, Germany

25 July, Unipol Arena, Bologna, Italy

26 July, Pala Alpitour, Turin, Italy

29 July, WiZink Center, Madrid, Spain

30 July, Altice Arena, Lisbon, Portugal


15/16 August, Scotiabank Arena, Toronto, Canada

20/21/22/26/27/28 August, Madison Square Garden, New York City, USA


1/2/3/7/8/10/14/15/21 September, Madison Square Garden, New York City, USA

22/26/28/29 September, Moody Center, Austin, USA


2/3 October, Moody Center, Austin, USA

8/9/10/13/14/15 October, United Center, Chicago, USA

23/24/26/28/29/31 October, Kia Forum, Inglewood, USA

2/9/11/12/14/15 November, Kia Forum, Inglewood, USA

Harry Styles performs onstage during his
Love On Tour, Chicago — 10 Oct. 2022

2/9/11/12/14/15 November, Kia Forum, Inglewood, USA

20 November, Arena VFG, Guadalajara, Mexico

22 November, Arena Monterray, Monterray, Mexico

24/25 November, Foro Sol, Mexico City, Mexico

27 November, Coliseo Live, Bogata, Colombia

29 November, Estadio Nacional, Lima, Peru

1 December, Estadio Bicentenario de La Florida,
Santiago, Chile

3/4 December, Estadio River Plate, Buenos Aires,
Argentina

6 December, Allianz Parque, Sao Paulo, Brazil

8 December, Jeunesse Arena, Rio de Janiero, Brazil

10 December, Pedreira Paulo Leminski, Curitiba,

13/14 December, Allianz Parque, Sao Paulo, Brazil

2023

26/27/29 January, Kia Forum, Inglewood, USA

31 January, Acrisure Arena, Thousand Palms, USA

1 February, Acrisure Arena, Thousand Palms, USA

20 February, HBF Park, Perth, Australia

24/25 February, Marvel Stadium, Melbourne, Australia

28 February, Metricon Stadium, Gold Coast, Australia

3-4 March, Accor Stadium, Sydney, Australia

7 March, Mount Smart Stadium, Auckland, New Zealand

11 March, Rajamangala Stadium, Bangkok, Thailand

14 March, Philippine Arena, Bulacan, Philippines

17 March, National Stadium, Singapore

20 March, KSPO Dome, Seoul, South Korea,

24/25 March, Ariake Arena, Tokyo, Japan

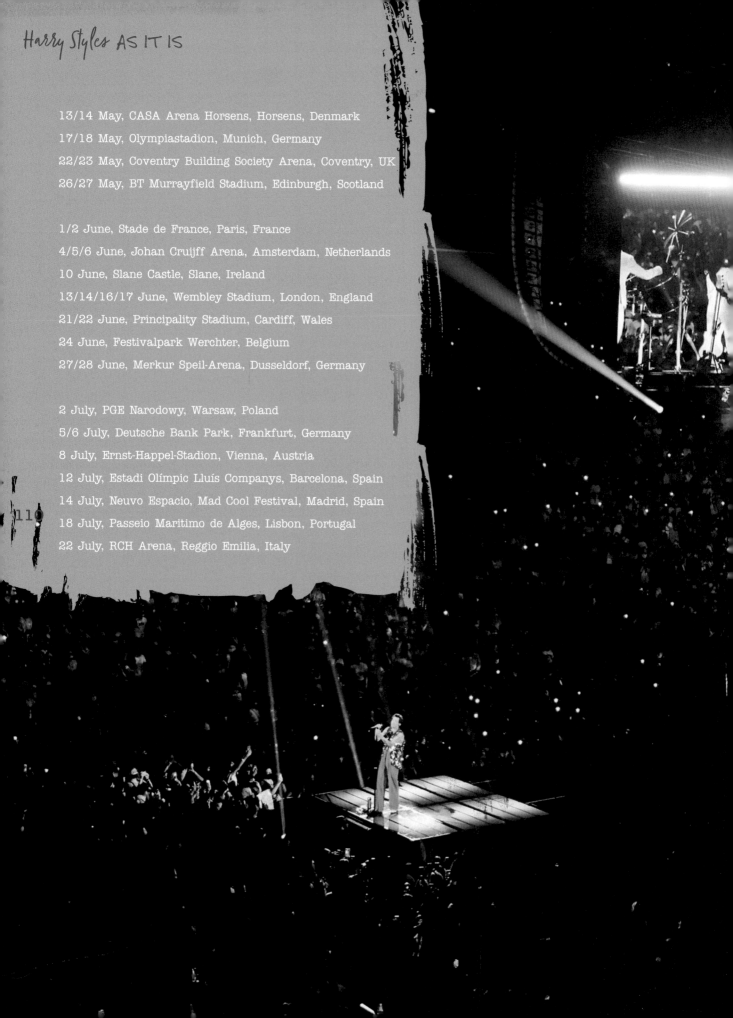

13/14 May, CASA Arena Horsens, Horsens, Denmark

17/18 May, Olympiastadion, Munich, Germany

22/23 May, Coventry Building Society Arena, Coventry, UK

26/27 May, BT Murrayfield Stadium, Edinburgh, Scotland

1/2 June, Stade de France, Paris, France

4/5/6 June, Johan Cruijff Arena, Amsterdam, Netherlands

10 June, Slane Castle, Slane, Ireland

13/14/16/17 June, Wembley Stadium, London, England

21/22 June, Principality Stadium, Cardiff, Wales

24 June, Festivalpark Werchter, Belgium

27/28 June, Merkur Speil-Arena, Dusseldorf, Germany

2 July, PGE Narodowy, Warsaw, Poland

5/6 July, Deutsche Bank Park, Frankfurt, Germany

8 July, Ernst-Happel-Stadion, Vienna, Austria

12 July, Estadi Olímpic Lluís Companys, Barcelona, Spain

14 July, Neuvo Espacio, Mad Cool Festival, Madrid, Spain

18 July, Passeio Maritimo de Alges, Lisbon, Portugal

22 July, RCH Arena, Reggio Emilia, Italy

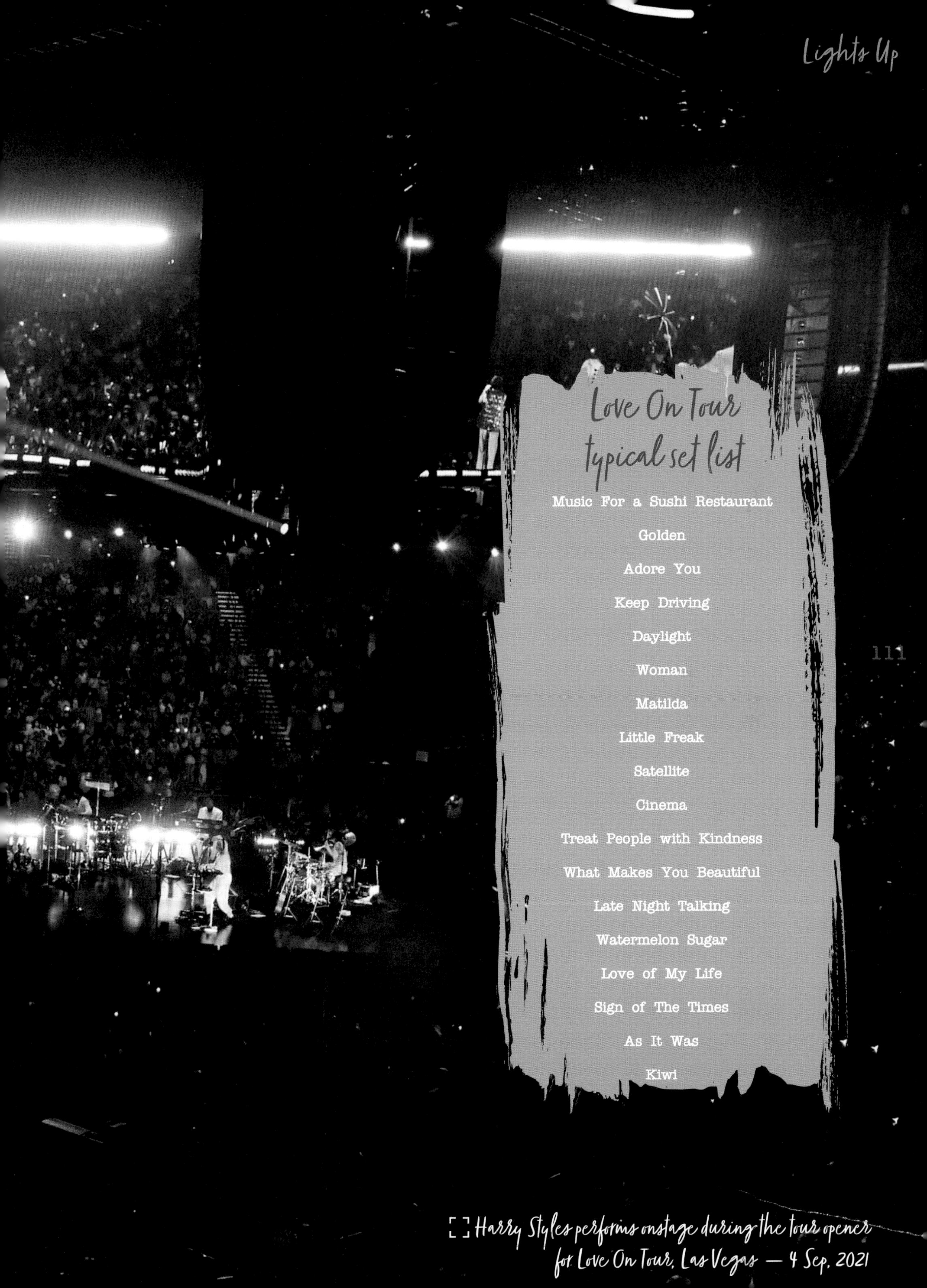

## Love On Tour
## typical set list

Music For a Sushi Restaurant

Golden

Adore You

Keep Driving

Daylight

Woman

Matilda

Little Freak

Satellite

Cinema

Treat People with Kindness

What Makes You Beautiful

Late Night Talking

Watermelon Sugar

Love of My Life

Sign of The Times

As It Was

Kiwi

111

[ ] Harry Styles performs onstage during the tour opener
for Love On Tour, Las Vegas — 4 Sep. 2021

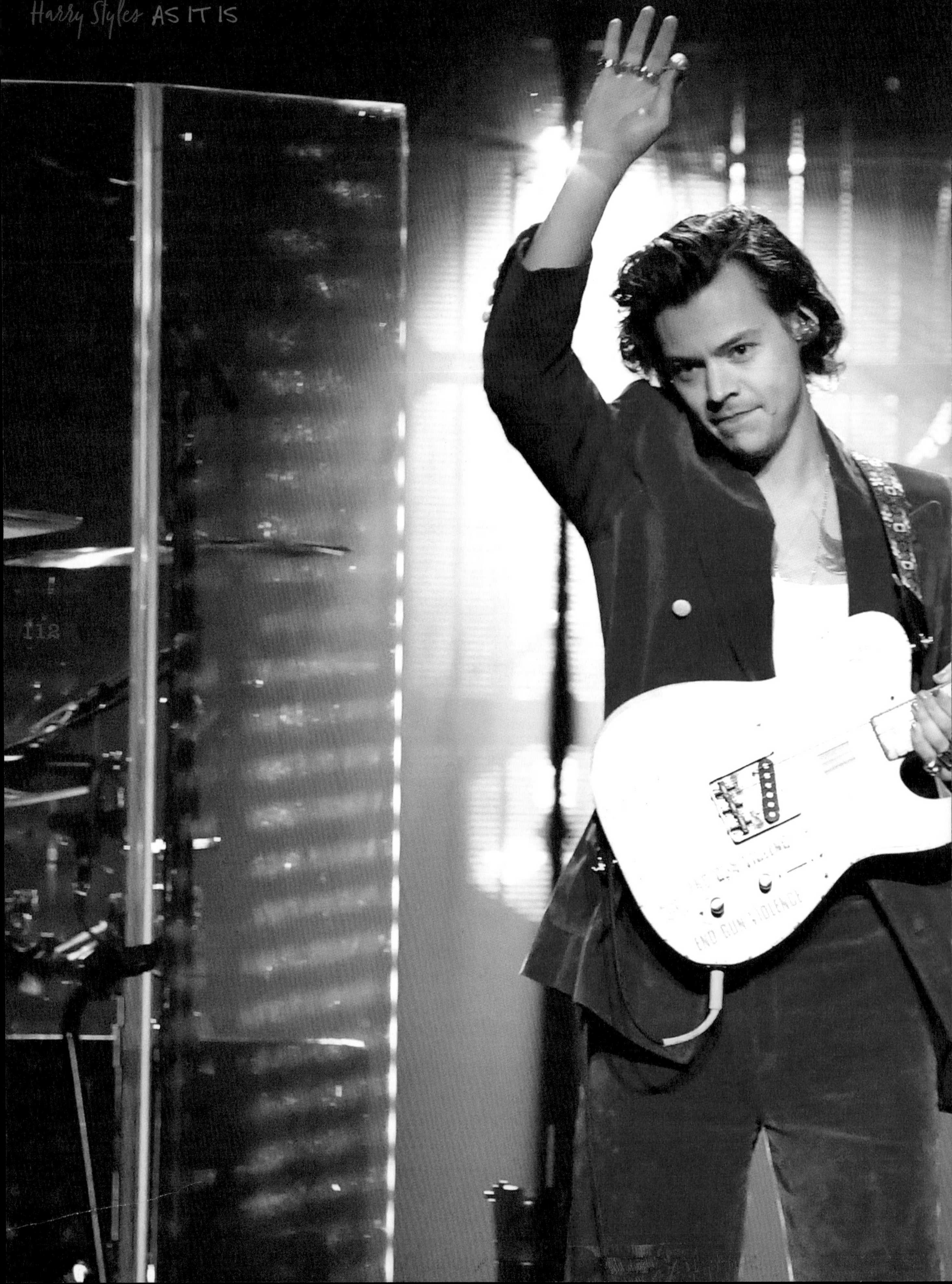
END GUN VIOLENCE

[ ] Harry Styles and Inductee Stevie Nicks perform at the 2019
Rock & Roll Hall Of Fame Induction Ceremony — Show at
Barclays Center, NYC — 29 March, 2019

113

114

Harry Styles attends the 2014 American Music
Awards at Nokia Theatre L.A. Live — 23 November, 2014

# Up All Night

## The women who've been wild about Harry

When you are one of the biggest pop stars on the planet, girlfriends are never hard to find. But Harry's success with women goes above and beyond the fact that he's rich, famous and handsome.

According to his nearest and dearest, Harry's genuine charm, thoughtful nature and cheeky grin made him a hit with girls, even before he was famous.

According to his sister Gemma, Harry had his first girlfriend at the age of four or five. Then White Eskimo band mate Will Sweeny told the Daily Star newspaper, 'I know it sounds funny but, even in primary school, he had a few girls on the go. It was rather amusing. From Year Four when he was about 10 Harry started with proper girlfriends. He just had this unbelievable way with girls all his life.'

A few years later Louis Tomlinson from 1D told The Sun. 'The only problem with sharing a flat with Harry is the constant stream of women he is getting through our door. It's relentless.'

Harry's first well-documented celebrity love affair was with Caroline Flack who presented the UK's X Factor companion after show 'The Xtra Factor' during the show's seventh season. The romance caused a media storm largely because of the age gap, Caroline was 31 and Harry 17.

The 'Haroline' relationship was brief — things turned sour when they went public. As Caroline told NME, "It began to go wrong when he was pictured coming out of my house one morning. And that was that. In the street people started shouting 'paedophile' at me in the street and 'pervert'.

115

In what was to become a gentlemanly pattern, Harry maintained a discreet silence over the whole affair. To this day he will not discuss any of his girlfriends.

But the press coverage about him and Caroline started the idea that he was a heartthrob and his love life — real or imagined — has continued to make headlines ever since as girl after girl is linked to him romantically by the media.

American model Emma Ostilly was next to be rumoured as being Harry's girl when the couple were spotted kissing in New Zealand. Emma did appear in One Direction's music video for Gotta Be You. British comic actor Emily Atack was another rumoured girlfriend in 2012, and went on to confirm the link in an interview with Reveal magazine a few years later. 'We were never girlfriend and boyfriend,' she said. 'We had a short-lived thing that was just a bit of fun. Then we went off in our opposite directions.' That same year Harry briefly dated reality star Caggie Dunlop of TV's Made in Chelsea fame.

116

However his next romance was sure to catapult him back into the gossip columns — towards the end of 2012 he was linked with Taylor Swift, one of the biggest music stars on the planet. Again their time together was brief but made a huge impact. Both Taylor and Harry have subsequently released music believed to be about their time together.

Taylor is well-known for writing 'break up tracks' about her previous relationships so it's not surprising that several of her tracks have been mentioned as possible Harry-related songs, including I Knew You Were Trouble, I Wish You Would, Style and Out of the Woods.

For his part Harry co-wrote the 2015 One Direction hit Perfect on the Made in the A.M. album which was thought to be about Taylor. It included the lyric, 'And if you're looking for someone to write your break-up songs about, baby I'm perfect'. More recently Two Ghosts on his Fine Line album included a description of a woman with 'Same lips red, same eyes blue' which got fans wondering if this was also a reference to Taylor.

[ ] Taylor Swift — 2013

## Wild about Harry romance timeline

**2011**
Caroline Flack

**2012**
Emma Ostilly
Emily Atack

**2013**
Taylor Swift
Kendall Jenner

**2014**
Actress Erin Foster, former stepsister
of Gigi and Bella Hadid.

**2015**
Victoria's Secret model Nadine Leopold
from Austria
Portuguese Victoria's Secret model
Sara Sampaio
Model Georgia Fowler from
New Zealand

117

**2015/16**
Kendall Jenner (again!)

**2016**
Fashion stylist Pandora Lennard

**2017**
Chef and food blogger Tess Ward

**2017-18**
Victoria's Secret model Camille Rowe —
he was pictured holding her handbag
— she was introduced to his family

**2019**
Model Kiko Mizuhara

**2020/22**
Olivia Wilde, actress and director

**2023**
Emily Ratajkowski, American model
and actress

Speaking about the speculation to Entertainment Today Harry said; 'I think the fun thing about music in general is that you write a lot of stuff from personal experience. It doesn't have to be literal and people can interpret a lot of different things in different ways. And I'm not going to tell someone it's not about what they think it's about because I think the whole point is it's about whatever it means to you.'

His relationship with Taylor ended in 2013 and although other names were in the mix that year including Kimberly Stewart (daughter of singer Rod Stewart) it seems Harry's next important relationship was with Kendall Jenner from the world's number one reality fame family, the Kardashians. They enjoyed an on/off relationship for a couple of years and are reportedly still friends, with Kendall rumoured to have inspired some of Harry's music.

Harry's gruelling work schedule makes any relationship a little difficult to manage and certainly some of his assumed 'affairs' have been short lived. He's been linked to several Victoria's Secret models, particularly Camille Rowe who was reportedly introduced to his family, as well as actress and writer Erin Foster, food blogger Tess Ward and fashion stylist Pandora Lennard.

Then came one of Harry's most serious relationships to date, his two-year love affair with American actress and director Olivia Wilde, who directed Harry's 2021 film Don't Worry Darling. Gossip columns were plump with news and views about their separation in November 2022, which most commentators described as 'amicable' and explained by Harry's extensive and lengthy 'Love on Tour' touring schedule. Certainly, their careers and personal lives were in very different places once filming and promotion for Olivia's film was finished. The track Cinema on Harry's House alludes to his relationship with Olivia in a rare and coded reference to his usually closely guarded romantic life.

During his Love on Tour series of concerts Harry was pictured with American model and actress Emily Ratajkowski. The starry pair were captured on camera getting cosy on the streets of Tokyo while in the Japanese capital for a stop on his world tour.

118

Being so close to his mother and sister should make Harry a great and attentive date who can appreciate what women want from their relationships. According to sister Gemma, Harry is a thoughtful soul. She remembers that when their mother was a single mum and had had a bad day, she and Harry would try to cheer her up as best they could. Even as a young teenager Harry would understand that a lovely bath is a huge treat and would organise that, all topped off with a selection of candles he'd gathered up from around the house.

But despite now having dated a long string of famous and high-profile women, Harry says little about any of them, preferring to let his music do the talking.

In fact he almost plays on sexual ambiguity himself — wearing pearls and nail polish and even dresses on occasion. He refuses all and any labels, seemingly equally comfortable with a pride flag on his arm as a good-looking model. An unreleased track Medicine which is popular when he sings it during concert performances, includes the lyric, 'The boys and the girls are in, I'll mess around with them and I'm OK with it.'

130

## He's on record as saying he'd like to be married one day.

Another of Harry's female fans — but totally platonic and professionally — is songwriter and Fleetwood Mac legend Stevie Nicks. The feeling is mutual, Harry is a massive fan of hers and was chosen to induct her into the Rock and Roll Hall of Fame in 2019 as a solo artist. She was the first female artist to be inducted for a second time — first with Fleetwood Mac and then for her solo work. On that occasion he described her as, 'everything you've ever wanted in a lady, in a lover, in a friend. She is a beacon to all of us. She's so wise and serene.'

For her part Stevie has described Harry as the 'son she never had' and told the crowd at a Fleetwood Mac concert in London, 'I'd like to dedicate this [song] to my little muse, Harry Styles, who brought his mother tonight. Her name is Anne. And I think you did a really good job raising Harry, Anne. Because he's really a gentleman, sweet and talented, and, boy, that appeals to me.'

121

123

Harry Styles performs during the Victoria's Secret
Fashion Show, Shanghai — 20 November, 2017

# That's what makes him beautiful

## Harry's hair and style

Harry's enthusiasm for fashion and style is second only to his love of music and he's become well known for his eclectic and gender-bending tastes.

He has come a long way from his 1D teenage days of t-shirts, low-slung jeans, track suits, beanie hats and a love of Jack Wills, to blossom into a fully-fledged fashion icon with an individual, high-end style all of his own. Knitwear, pastels, pearls, polka dots, feathers, fur, fluorescent acids, prints – there's really nothing that's too fantastical in Harry's world.

'Harry's sense of style is so unique' said fashion designer Daniel Fletcher, writing about Harry's appearance in British GQ magazine's Best Dressed list.

'He's fearless and I love that about him. His ability to blur gender boundaries and embrace his femininity, without looking like he's thought twice about it, is absolutely unparalleled.'

Designer Michael Kors called Harry 'the modern embodiment of British rocker style, edgy, flamboyant and worn with unapologetic swagger'.

Harry was announced as the face of Gucci in 2018 and wore custom-made outfits by their designer Alessandro Michele for his 'Harry Styles on Tour' shows. He is also a fan of Saint Laurent, Burberry, Calvin Klein, Givenchy, Raf Simons and Alexander McQueen.

Harry also made the best-dressed list compiled by Esquire magazine in 2021. Describing him as the 'maximalist master', the magazine praised the fact that he seems to have so much fun '...with his clothes...and nails and everything else'.

[ ] Harry Styles attends the 'Dunkirk' World Premiere at
Odeon Leicester Square, London — 13 July, 2017

125

# Putting the style into Harry Styles – Introducing stylist Harry Lambert

Nowadays, as one of the most famous men on the planet, Harry naturally has some help with his look.

The man behind most of the singer's most arresting looks, and responsible for helping Harry Styles become, as the New York Times puts it, 'a fearlessly androgynous fashion plate,' is another Harry, fashion stylist Harry Lambert.

Working together has seen the two 'Harrys' become a boundary-pushing fashion force to be reckoned with. Lambert's approach to styling Harry Styles is to create looks that are bold, daring, and unconventional, yet always effortlessly cool. Lambert has played a crucial role in defining and refining Harry's image and androgynous style.

Lambert has dressed Harry in everything from flamboyant printed suits to gender-bending ensembles that challenge traditional notions of masculinity. He has also collaborated with top fashion designers, including Gucci's Alessandro Michele, to create custom outfits for Styles' performances and appearances.

One of Lambert's standout styling moments with Harry was at the 2021 Grammy Awards, where the singer wore a Gucci leather suit with a feather boa and matching green-tinted sunglasses. The statement look was bold and daring. Perfectly capturing Harry's unique style and personality, it quickly became one of the most talked-about looks of the night.

126

Harry Styles attends The 2019 Met Gala Celebrating Camp: Notes on Fashion at Metropolitan Museum of Art. NYC — 6 May, 2019

127

According to Harry's sister Gemma, the signs of his passion for fashion were always there. 'As a 'cool' kid, Harry stood out but also fitted in,' she told Another Man magazine. 'He was always interested in clothes and spent all of his birthday money and wages on getting the train into Manchester to expand his wardrobe. He had a paper round and then worked in the bakery in the village for a while. I'd barely be eating my cereal by the time he got home from these absurdly early jobs — the pull of new trainers obviously outweighing time in bed.

'As a wave of emo teenagers took over Holmes Chapel, we both caught the bug with our floppy fringes and studded belts. To get the look he tried stealing my straighteners to attack his curls — and failed, enlisting my help to smooth his hair into submission. Later, he let me cut it as well: I had no idea what I was doing and he'd always hate it for the first 20 minutes before admitting I was right and it did look better. The skinny jeans never went away... but the chequered pumps did.'

Harry himself supplied another clue to his early influences when he told Entertainment Tonight, 'I think both music and fashion, [my] main influence was probably Shania Twain.... I think she's amazing'.

He's also on record endorsing the famous quote from Clash bassist Paul Simonon saying; 'Pink is the only true rock and roll colour'.

Nowadays as one of the most famous men on the planet, Harry naturally has some help with his look. He is a major client of another 'Harry' — fashion stylist Harry Lambert is the man behind most of the singer's major appearances.

## Tattoos

Harry has more than 50 intricate tattoos on his body ranging from large to very small. Covering them all up for his acting roles can take up to an hour in make up. 'It's the only time I really regret getting tattooed' he said in an interview with Variety.

### Harry's inkings include:

- ➤ Two Swallows facing each other on his chest
- ➤ A butterfly on his upper stomach
- ➤ Two fern leaves on his lower stomach
- ➤ A skeleton dressed in a suit on his left upper arm
- ➤ A rose on his left lower arm
- ➤ A naked mermaid and a 'You Booze You Lose' and bottle of alcohol on his left forearm
- ➤ An eagle on his right arm
- ➤ Various initials and dates relating to beloved family members
- ➤ Brazil! tattoo on thigh during his stay there as part of Love on Tour in December 2022

Amid the body art, fans have spotted that Harry has four nipples, two supernumerary ones located beneath his two regularly placed ones.

130

## Jewellery

If 50 plus tattoos weren't adornment enough, Harry also has a penchant for pendants, earrings and rings. From the XXL drop pearl earring he wore at the Met gala in 2019 to the gold chains on the cover of Fine Line, Harry's pieces once again, never fail to make the headlines.

## Harry loves:

✝ His signature string of pearls necklace

✝ Talisman cross-shaped pendant necklace

✝ Senna necklace — a chain made of colourful beads with floral designs, interspersed with freshwater pearls, made by Eliou

✝ Blue Millefiori glass beaded choker

✝ Custom-made, chunky initial letter H and S gold Gucci rings

Pictures of Harry in a string of pearls flew around the world in 2019. He also hosted the annual fund-raising Met Gala in New York that year, one of the fashion industry's biggest events, causing a stir by appearing on the red carpet dressed in a sheer black Gucci jumpsuit, with a ruffled collar and embroidered sleeves.

In December 2020 he became the first man to appear solo on the cover of Vogue. The photograph of him wearing a Gucci gown made headlines and cemented his position as the high priest of fashion- forward, flamboyant and fun designs.

'To not wear [something] because it's female's clothing, you shut out a whole world of great clothes. What's exciting about right now is that you can wear what you like ….. the lines are becoming more and more blurred,' Harry said of the appearance.

Tom Lamont of The Guardian said some of Harry's fashion choices have contributed to 'an important political discussion about gendered fashion'. Harry told him; ' In terms of how I want to dress… I tend to make decisions in terms of collaborators I want to work with. I want things to look a certain way. Not because it makes me look gay, or it makes me look straight, or it makes me look bisexual, but just because I think it looks cool.'

131

Speaking to People magazine about Harry's style, Olivia Wilde, his one-time girlfriend and director of his latest film Don't Worry Darling said; 'I did a little victory dance when we heard that we officially had Harry in the film, because we knew that he has a real appreciation for fashion and style, and this movie is incredibly stylistic. It's very heightened and opulent and I'm really grateful that he is so enthusiastic about that element of the process — some actors just don't care.

'To me he is very modern and I hope that this brand of confidence as a male that Harry has — truly devoid of any traces of toxic masculinity — is indicative of his generation and therefore the future of the world. It's pretty powerful and kind of extraordinary to see someone in his position redefining what it can mean to be a man with confidence'.

Not all Harry's looks are gender-fluid though. He rocks a tailored suit, and according to one Harry-watcher has at least 1,000 patterned suits to his name. As a headline in Vogue once described him; 'Harry Styles Looks Like a Glam Rock God in Gucci'.

132

## The Mane Man

Harry's hair is the focus of huge publicity. Long and curly or short and slick, his hair gets plenty of attention.

It's obvious that he enjoys experimenting with different looks, but also that he realises that hair is an important part of his image and deserves the appropriate care and attention. British Vogue magazine took a look at his dressing table backstage during a show in Paris and counted seven hair products, including several from celebrity hair care line Ouai.

Harry Styles while with One Direction, onstage during 102.7 KIIS FM Jingle Ball, at Staples Center, LA — 4 December 4, 2015

133

## The Style Files
## Harry Loves:

- Silk scarves
- Printed shirts
- Brocade suits
- Tuxedo jackets
- Flared trousers
- Baggy trousers
- Wyatt boots
- Gucci's Mémoire d'une Odeur — a genderless designer fragrance for which Harry is the official face.
- Tom Ford Tobacco Vanille, Diptyque candles
- Sunday Riley facial oil.

134

Naturally the time would come for Harry to have his own beauty range – and the day dawned in November 2021 when his gender-neutral, vegan and cruelty-free Pleasing brand was launched.

'When we decided Pleasing would make beauty products I wanted to be sure they were something I would use,' Harry said. 'I didn't want to make products to mask people, I wanted to highlight them and make them feel beautiful.'

Initially comprising four nail polishes, a dual roller ball lip and eye serum, and a facial serum, the range is inspired by Harry's favourite pearls. All the nail polishes are named accordingly, the white is Perfect Pearl, the pale pink is Granny's Pearls, the navy/black is Inky Pearl, and the clear topcoat is called Pearly Tops. Accompanied by a set of black and white nail stickers, customers can create a mismatched manicure just as Harry does his. Even the serum is delivered in a bottle filled with white pearl-style capsules.

135

With the brand aiming to celebrate 'the multitude of unique identities in our community', the promotion material includes models of all genders.

# Golden Boy
## Harry's acting career, film and tv appearances

Like other musicians with charisma and swagger, such as Mick Jagger and David Bowie, Harry looks set to juggle his love of music with forays into the world of acting.

His first 'acting' appearance was in a 2012 episode of Nickelodeon's iCarly show, along with the rest of One Direction. The boys all performed as themselves, although the plot centered on Harry, who, just before the band were due to perform, drank out of lead character Carly's water bottle and caught 'jungle worms'. A doctor had previously warned Carly that she was contagious and shouldn't kiss anybody. Even after he's recovered, Harry insists that he still has the 'worms' so that Carly will keep taking care of him.

136

As well as making his acting debut in Dunkirk as a serious actor in a major movie, Harry's also shown comedic flair and demonstrated a talent for presenting. He can think on his feet quickly enough to host prime time American talk shows and has guest-hosted both Saturday Night Live and James Corden's Late Late Show to great acclaim in the USA.

Speaking afterwards about how he appeared so calm during his appearance on the American institution that is Saturday Night Live, Harry said; 'SNL was the calmest I've been for anything, I don't really know why. I used to get so nervous before everything to the point that I'd almost always be really disappointed because I was too nervous.'

As for the future, Harry has said; 'I don't see myself as wanting to go get a movie because I have a year off. It needs to be something I really want to do.'

[ ] Harry Styles during a photo-call in Dunkirk, ahead of the release of the movie "Dunkirk", Dunkerque, France — 16 July, 2017

# Dunkirk

Harry made his big-screen debut in the 2017 smash hit movie Dunkirk, alongside a starry ensemble cast including Kenneth Branagh, Cillian Murphy, Mark Rylance and Tom Hardy.

The film tells the story of the evacuation of the beaches and harbour of Dunkirk during the Second World War. Harry played 'Alex', a young British soldier who is saved from the ocean after his ship is sunk.

Crazy times then ensue. Harry spends most of his time soaked through but still very handsome. He had to chop off his famous long curls in favour of a 'short at the sides' look in order to play the part of a 1940s soldier, but fans loved the new style.

Actors Tom Glynn-Carney, Fionn Whitehead, Producer Emma Thomas, Director Christopher Nolan, Actors Harry Styles and Jack Lowden pose for "Dunkirk" Photocall. Dunkerque, France — 16 July, 2017

"I was so excited to be in the movie that I didn't think too much about it,' Harry said of his haircut afterwards. 'I assumed when auditioning for a movie that was set in World War ll ...I'd imagined that I'd probably have to have a trim. It was a little breezy behind the ears, which was nice'.

Dunkirk's director Christopher Nolan, who cast Harry ahead of thousands of other auditionees, says he didn't really realise quite how famous Harry was at the time. 'I mean my daughter had talked about him, my kids had talked about him, but I wasn't really

139

that aware of it. So the truth is I cast Harry because he fit the part wonderfully and truly earned a seat at the table.'

Not that Harry spent much time sitting around during the film. His character nearly drowns as the boat which rescued him is then also hit and water floods into its lower decks.

Abandoning ship for a second time and struggling in the ocean he is then refused entry to a paddleboat because its passengers fear it will capsize if he climbs aboard. He eventually makes it back to shore and, after other adventures including exposing a foreign spy, eventually makes it back to Britain.

Film critic Robbie Collin praised Harry for a 'bright, convicted and unexpectedly not-at-all-jarring performance'.

His approach to the role and advance preparation was quite straightforward. 'Someone told me "say the words like it's the first time you're saying them". So I thought I'd make it so it really was the first time I was saying them. I learned them but didn't say them out loud before filming the scene.'

During an appearance on British morning show 'This Morning' Harry said that he found auditioning for Christopher Nolan was more daunting than singing for Simon Cowell. 'He doesn't say anything. Like at all. He just sits in the darkness in the back of the room... It's so intense because you do the audition and go home and kind of obsess over whether people liked you or not.'

Although already used to appearing in huge stadiums around the world, even Harry was at first taken aback by the sheer scale of the production of this big-budget war epic.

Speaking to USA Today during promotion for the movie, Harry said; 'While you're down there [in the water] filming and acting out the scene, you're also thinking, "I cannot breathe for much longer than this," which obviously helps the situation.

140

'We all, along with the crew, were just getting rest when we could. They didn't put us in heated tents or anything like that between scenes. You were out there still. It really stripped you down to your bare bones. It made the whole film kind of come out in its rawest form.

'I really enjoyed it. Absolutely. It's so different to try and completely remove yourself from a situation and be someone else. It was something new for me. Even with the drowning scenes, I quite enjoyed it, to be honest. I'd do it again.'

# Eternals (2021)

Harry surprised fans when he popped up in the post credits scene of Marvel Studio's Eternals movie as Eros, also known as Starfox, the brother of Thanos, and a fellow Prince of Titan. Harry caused a massive buzz in the Marvel fandom with everyone eager to see him entering the Marvel universe more fully in later films.

141

# CBeebies Bedtime Story (2022)

Ahead of the autumn 2022 releases of his more mainstream movies Don't Worry Darling and My Policeman, Harry made an appearance on the BBC children's tv channel CBeebies, reading a story in the popular 7pm bedtime story slot on 23 May 2022.

His choice was the picture book 'In Every House, On Every Street' by Jess Hitchman, which he read while sitting in a yellow chair wearing cosy brown Gucci pyjamas, polka dotted with blue, and accessorised with a string of blue beads around his neck.

### Netflix and chill

When Harry has a cosy night in he will usually opt to watch a romantic comedy.

But he says his overall favourite film is tear-jerker love story The Notebook.

142

# Don't Worry Darling (2022)

Harry's second film is Don't Worry Darling' — a psychological thriller, set in an isolated, utopian community in the 1950s Californian desert. It premiered at the prestigious Venice film festival in September 2022.

Shooting took place between September 2020 and February 2021 in LA and Palm Springs. Harry had to stay put during that time because of the Covid rules and so it became the longest time he had lived in one place in 11 years, since his time in One Direction.

He plays 'Jack' a character said to 'love his wife dearly but hiding a dark secret from her'. He is also credited as a songwriter in the music department of the film, according to the IMDbPro website.

Directed, produced and starring Olivia Wilde, the film's other main stars along with Harry, are Florence Pugh and Chris Pine. 'It's a great cast,' Chris told Harper's Bazaar magazine. 'Harry Styles is an absolute delight .. one of the most professional people I've ever met. He couldn't be kinder, more gracious, I mean really I was stunned by this kid. He's off-the-charts cool'

Describing his experiences as an actor in an interview with Rolling Stone magazine, Harry commented on the difference between movies and music production. 'In music, there's such an immediate response to what you do. You finish a song and people clap. When you're filming and they say "cut" there's maybe part of you that expects everyone to start clapping [but] they don't. Everyone, obviously, goes back to do their jobs and you're like ...was that bad?'.

[ ] Harry Styles arrives for the screening of the film "Don't Worry Darling", Venice, Italy — 5 Sep. 2022

[ ] Harry Styles seen on the film set for 'My Policeman'. Brighton, England — 14 May, 2021

144

# My Policeman (2022)

Just a few weeks after finishing 'Don't Worry Darling', Harry got to work on another film, My Policeman. He played the part of Tom, a policeman who develops feelings for a museum curator called Patrick. It's all set in the 1950s when homosexuality was illegal in the UK, so the couple keep their affair a secret. 'It's obviously unfathomable now to think "Oh you couldn't be gay, that was illegal" Harry told Rolling Stone magazine. 'I think everyone, including myself, has their own journey with figuring out sexuality and getting more comfortable with it'.

The film premiered at the Toronto International Film Festival in September 2022 and had a limited cinema run before its streaming release in November.

145

Harry Styles and Emma Corrin speak onstage at the "My Policeman" Press Conference during the Toronto International Film Festival — 11 Sep. 2022

# Millennial celebrity
## Being famous in the 21st century

The odds of any 16-year-old from Worcestershire becoming famous worldwide are billions to one. So it's only natural that Harry would sit back sometimes and consider how it happened for him.

'I think about it all the time,' he told US interviewer Howard Stern in a 2020 interview in support of Fine Line. 'It reminds me how lucky I am. I know there are hundreds of thousands, if not millions, who are far superior musicians to me but not everyone gets to do it. Sometimes we make our own luck, but so much of it is about luck and timing. There's no reason for it to have been me.'

Through all the fame and attendant madness, Harry has seemingly managed to keep his feet on the ground. It's helped that Harry has always felt loved and supported by both his parents, and step-parents.

But additionally he made a move just as One Direction were becoming well-known which he says was one of the best decisions of his life. Instead of rushing to get his own luxury penthouse pad, Harry moved into the family home of Ben Winston, a producer he hadn't known for long then, but who has been described as a 'friendly mentor' to Harry. This allowed him to fly under the radar a little as no one was expecting to find him in suburban north London in between gigs on the other side of the world.

Harry moved in for a planned two weeks but the stay turned into 18 months. 'It was great', said Harry, who believes this is what kept him grounded as his life turned upside down. 'It was probably the best move I ever made.'

Having arrived in London, away from his family, and entering the 1D whirlwind aged

[ ] Harry while with One Direction on stage at BIC.
Bournemouth, UK — 3 January, 2012

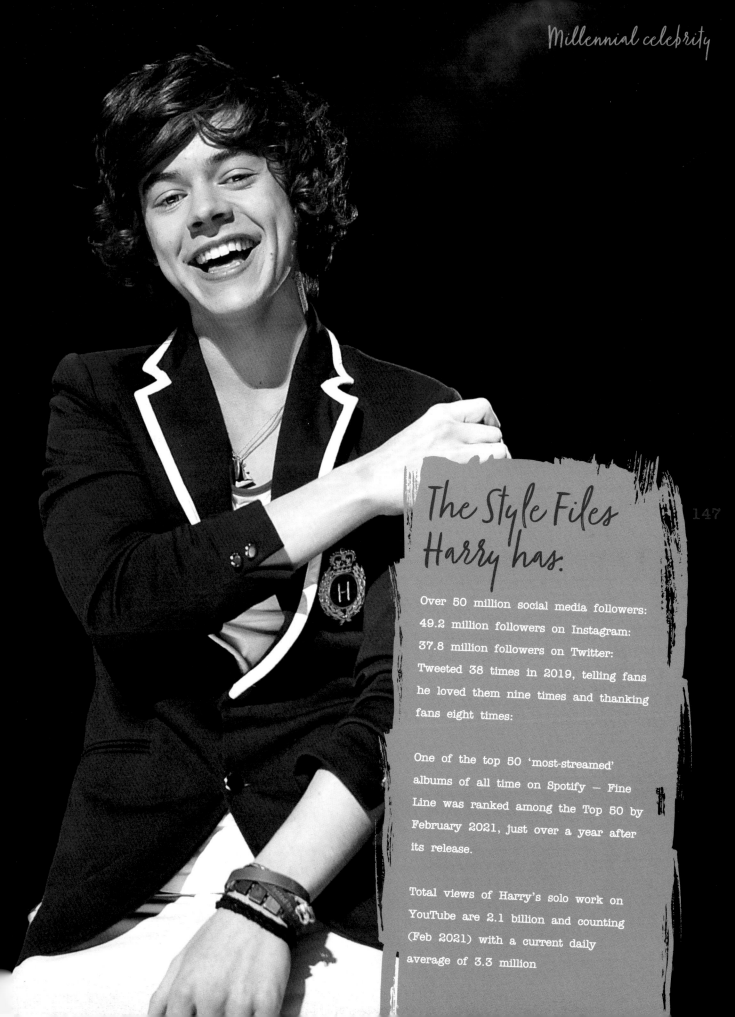

## The Style Files
## Harry has:

Over 50 million social media followers:
49.2 million followers on Instagram:
37.8 million followers on Twitter:
Tweeted 38 times in 2019, telling fans
he loved them nine times and thanking
fans eight times:

One of the top 50 'most-streamed'
albums of all time on Spotify — Fine
Line was ranked among the Top 50 by
February 2021, just over a year after
its release.

Total views of Harry's solo work on
YouTube are 2.1 billion and counting
(Feb 2021) with a current daily
average of 3.3 million

147

148

[ ] Harry Styles performs on stage during Radio 1's Big Weekend 2022, Coventry, England — 29 May, 2022

Harry Styles attends the 2017 iHeartRadio Music Festival at T-Mobile Arena on, Las Vegas — 22 Sep, 2017

150

just 16, suddenly there were no rules. Many kids would have gone off the rails. But Harry was able to keep a feeling of family by living with Ben's family. After the whirl of X-Factor, he had some rules again. This was all happening right at the time he started going out in London and drinking and being offered drugs. But because Harry felt he didn't know the family, particularly Ben's wife, well enough to go back to their house worse for wear, he managed to avoid some of the worst excesses which trip up other young stars.

One of Harry's most useful coping mechanisms is in his ability to switch off when he's not working. 'I like to separate my personal life and work', Harry has explained. 'It helps, I think , for me to compartmentalise. It's not about trying to make my career longer, like trying to be this "mysterious character" because I'm not. When I go home I feel like the same person I was at school. You can't expect to keep that if you show everything.'

Social media has been a huge factor in music promotion since the early days of One Direction. It's a sophisticated operation now, used to great effect in the promotion of the single Adore You when his team created the fictional island of Eroda which fans worked out was the word Adore written backwards.

#VisitEroda was shared on social media, and the 'island' also had a website and FaceBook and Twitter accounts.

Fake or real – news about Harry buzzes around the globe 24/7. A good example of his incredible reach came in 2020 when a HarryStylesCardigan hashtag was so popular that it got 23.7 million hits on TikTok during lockdown. The hashtag has gone on to receive 40.1 million views to-date.

Harry had been shown wearing a colourful oversized patchwork woollen JW Anderson cardigan during a soundcheck ahead of a performance on the Today Show in America. Within a few days the video reached more than three million views and gained one

151

152

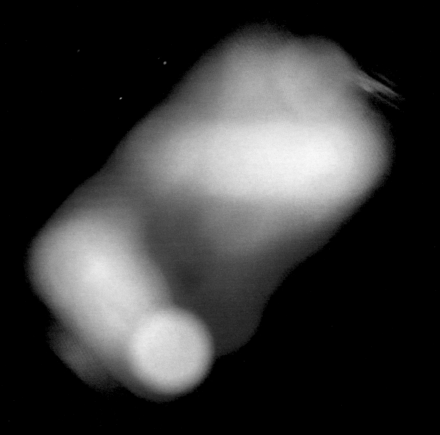

153

million 'likes'. Once it had gone viral, fans were keen to try to make the cardigan for themselves. Founder of JW Anderson, Jonathan Anderson was so amazed that he released the pattern for the cardigan free of charge, commenting that; 'I am so impressed and incredibly humbled by the trend and everyone knitting the cardigan. I really wanted to show our appreciation, so we are sharing the pattern with everyone. Keep it up!' The cardigan reached such heights of fame that it is now joining the fashion collection curated by the Victoria and Albert Museum in London.

None of Harry's musical influences back in the 1970s could have dreamt of achieving that type of reach via the print media that traditionally promoted stars in those days.

But such constant attention can be a curse, particularly because Harry's personal freedom is so important to him. He accepts a security detail when he is working, but prefers not to have it in his free time. 'It's uncomfortable', he told Howard Stern in an interview. 'A lot of the time you end up drawing more attention to yourself if you are walking in a city with some big guy behind you.'

154

He enjoys walking alone, listening to music, but on one occasion in America he was mugged at knifepoint for his phone. Luckily the altercation was interrupted before getting too nasty and Harry was ok. It's not even clear that the muggers realised who he was. However Harry was determined the doubtless chilling experience wouldn't let it stop him enjoying some normality when he could and so he went out walking the very next night because it's something he really enjoys and wants to continue to do.

It's this streak of 'normal' — along with a dry sense of humour — that keeps Harry grounded. Despite having been globally famous for more than 13 years now, he seems unexpectedly easy with all the attention. He charms awkward interviewers, bedazzles his fans, fascinates the media, confounds his critics and is respected by his peers — all while keeping his distinctive style.

He just seems to 'get' what's needed to stay sane as a 21st century celebrity. As Louise Bruton wrote in a review of his show in the Irish Times;

'[Harry] proves his superstar status easily, but he maintains a sincere level of modesty throughout the entire show, making him more personable than a lot of his pop star peers'

## Harry's tweets of kindness and love

Harry only tweets when he has something meaningful to say and never for the sake of it. He's very aware of mental health and how it can be adversely affected by social media. But he is also aware of what powerful platforms it can provide to spread kindness and love.

## A few of his tweets demonstrate this.

155

### 10 October 2019
World Mental Health Day

Go to therapy, it's important. I'll wait for you

### 23 July 2020
celebrating the 10th anniversary of One Direction becoming a band

I've been struggling to put into words how grateful I am for everything that's happened over the past 10 years. I've seen things and places that I'd only ever dreamt of when I was growing up.

### 3 July 2022
when Harry's concert was cancelled following a mass shooting in a shopping mall in Copenhagen

I'm heartbroken along with the people of Copenhagen. I adore this city... I'm devastated for the victims, their families, and everyone hurting. I'm sorry we couldn't be together. Please look after each other.

156

Harry Styles performs on the Coachella stage with Lizzo during the Coachella Valley Music And Arts Festival, Indio, California — 22 April, 2022

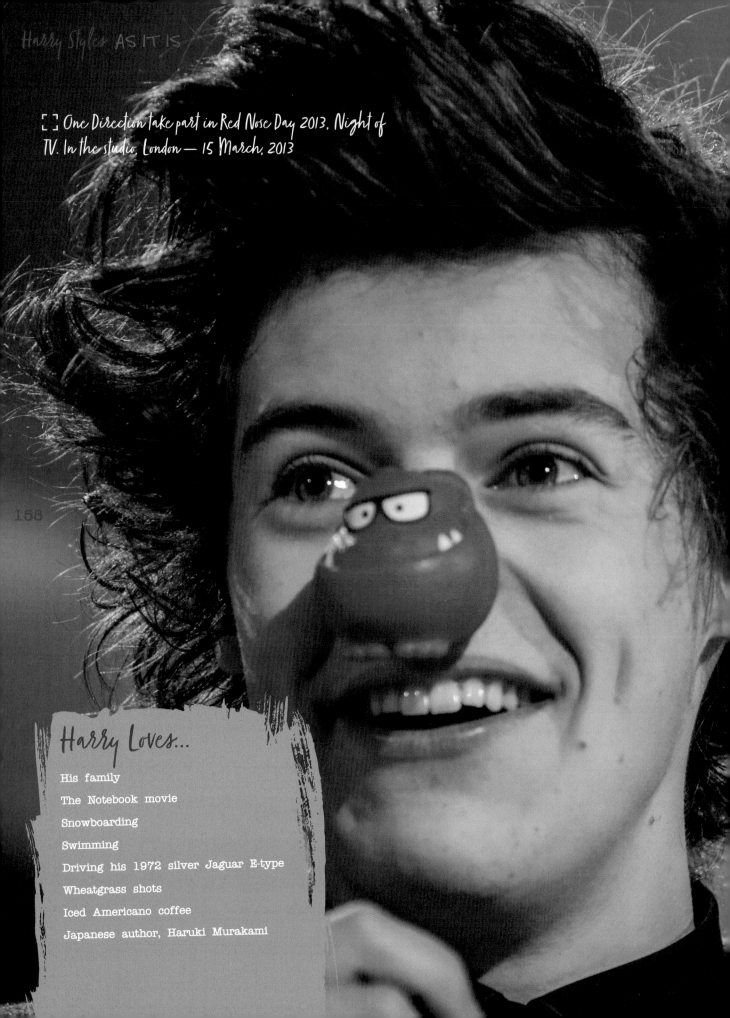

[ ] One Direction take part in Red Nose Day 2013. Night of TV. In the studio. London — 15 March, 2013

158

## Harry Loves...

His family

The Notebook movie

Snowboarding

Swimming

Driving his 1972 silver Jaguar E-type

Wheatgrass shots

Iced Americano coffee

Japanese author, Haruki Murakami

# Treating people with kindness

## Harry's charitable work and altruistic side

It's obvious that Harry is keen to use his talent and celebrity power to make a positive difference to the world.

Most recently he has pulled his ideas together under the Treat People With Kindness banner — abbreviated to TPWK — which now appears on his merchandise. As well as various T-shirts and hair ties, memorabilia available includes posters, sweaters, hats and hoodies. He also sold Pride T-shirts sold to raise funds for the GLSEN charity which aims to create a better world for LGBTQ students.

Treat People With Kindness is also the name of the eleventh track on Harry's Fine Line album and the sixth to be released as a single. It came out in January 2021, supported by a video featuring actress and writer Phoebe Waller-Bridge.

But Harry's support for many charities and good causes goes back many years. In February 2013 he and the other members of One Direction got involved with Comic Relief, recording that year's charity single One Way Or Another (Teenage Kicks) — their third UK #1, although all profits went to charity.

160

[ ] A Harry Styles signed Gibson Guitar, estimated between $3,000-5,000, on display at Julien's Auctions on September 1, 2020, Beverly Hills, ahead of the September 9 Recording Academy Musicares Charity Relief Auction

# The Style Files

According to the Look to the Stars website which records celebrity charity work, Harry has supported the following charities:

## Aid Still Required
Bringing attention to humanitarian aid for natural disasters or human crises

## Alzheimer's Society
Supporting people affected by dementia

## Amnesty International
Focused on human rights

## Born this Way Foundation
Committed to supporting the wellness of young people and empowering them to create a kinder, braver world

## Everytown
working to end gun violence in America

## Muhammad Ali Center
International museum and cultural centre promoting respect, hope and understanding

## MusiCares
Helping musicians in times of financial, personal or medical crisis

## Nordoff Robbins
The UK's largest music therapy charity

## Save the Children
Dedicated to improving the lives of children through better education, health care and economic opportunities, as well as providing emergency aid for natural disasters, wars and conflicts

## Trekstock
Offering practical and social support for young adults with cancer in the UK

161

As part of their involvement with the event that year the band visited Ghana, West Africa to see how the charity was helping the country's poorest people. As part of their visit, the 1D boys met children suffering with Aids and malaria and were visibly upset as they saw the terrible and fatal effects of the diseases first hand.

Harry was filmed breaking down in tears after meeting a three-year-old boy suffering with malaria and anaemia in the emergency department of a paediatric clinic due to benefit from Comic Relief funds.

His world tour 'Harry Styles: Live on Tour' raised $1.2 million in charitable donations as profits from merchandise, as well as a portion of ticket sales, were donated to various local charities from his tour stops around the world.

A total of 62 charities across Europe, America, Asia and Australia benefitted, including many supporting children, cancer, refugees and others working to eradicate hunger, homelessness and poverty.

He is all for inclusivity, often wearing a Pride flag and exhorting his fans to be 'whoever it is you want to be in this room tonight'. He promotes love and equality for all every chance he gets.

Reviewing one of Harry's shows for Esquire magazine Matt Miller complimented Harry's sensitivity around inclusivity, saying that the star reminds everyone that 'youths are here, they're aware, and they actually care.'

In an Instagram post clearing up confusion over a perceived lack of acknowledgment of a Black Lives Matter flag thrown on to the stage, Harry wrote to his fans; 'I love every single one of you. If you

[ ] Harry Styles while with One Direction performs at the 99.7 NOW! Triple Ho Show at SAP Center, San Jose, California — 2 December, 2015

163

## Lopping off his locks

Harry's long wavy hair was beyond shoulder-length in 2016 when he went for the chop.

He then donated his famous locks to a fabulous cause — a charity called the Little Princess Trust which uses real hair to make wigs for children who lose their hair, usually during cancer treatment. After reading the news of Harry's decision on social media accounts, his fans also got behind the charity and pledged generous donations themselves.

164

are black, if you are white. If you are gay, if you are straight, if you are transgender. Whoever you are, whoever you want to be. I support you. I love every single one of you.' During the tour Harry frequently waved Pride, Bi and Trans flags, as well as the BLM flag.

Following the chemical explosion at the port in Beirut, Lebanon in 2020 which killed more than 180 people, injured more than 5,000 and displaced a further 250,000 people, Harry donated to the Impact Lebanon charity established to help the casualties and rebuild the damage. He tweeted a link and implored his followers to make a donation themselves.

But it also seems he is still searching for a special cause to champion himself. Speaking to The Guardian in December 2019 after being asked why he didn't use his influence more than he does, Harry responded by saying he didn't want to dilute the effect he might have.

'Because I'd prefer, when I say something, for people to think I mean it. To be honest, I'm still searching for that one thing, you know? Something I can really stand up for, and get behind, and be like' "This is my Life Fight".

'There's a power to doing the one thing. You want your whole weight behind it.'

167

Harry Styles performs onstage during the 5th annual
"We Can Survive" benefit concert presented by CBS Radio
at the Hollywood Bowl, LA — 21 October, 2017

# What Next?

As the hottest pop star on the planet, Harry still has masses of energy and enthusiasm for his work - be that making music or movies. But surely after the mammoth undertaking of Love on Tour he'll have some time off.

Yet he's already said he's working on a fourth album and took time out in between his Love on Tour concerts to fit in some studio time for writing and recording. Harry has said that he's 'always writing' and he and the team are already throwing ideas around for the next album. 'All of us are excited to get back to it, which seems insane as we've just put an album out' he told Rolling Stone magazine. As a magnetic and compelling live performer, another tour would certainly be on the cards to promote new music.

He's also sure to continue with his blossoming acting career - with rumours abounding that he's joining the Marvel Eternals franchise.

One other source of intense speculation is over a reunion with One Direction. The smart money says he's too busy and successful to join any such venture. But he did get 1D fans in a lather when he posted and quickly deleted a photograph of himself in a 1D T-shirt shortly after publicly thanking the other members of the band when he collected his 2023 Grammy. Harry's explanation for the speedy removal of the post, was that he had intended to post it to his close friends, and not on his main account.

Harry has spoken of a reunion, saying on the Spout podcast, 'I'd love for there to be a time where it felt like something we all wanted to do. I very much enjoyed [the albums] and I think we all went through something really special together. There's a lot of love there. So, yeah, I think if there's a moment for us to do in the right way, I think it would be great.'

But if and until then, Harry reigns supreme as one of very few musicians to graduate from a boyband to become a successful solo artist.

Reflecting on his success, Harry said, 'I've always felt incredibly lucky to get to do this as my job … and I feel like I'm falling more and more in love with making music each time I get to do it.'

Harry gives 100 per cent to his music and his fans. As his career continues it looks certain there's more powerful work still to come.

169

[ ] Harry Styles performs on stage during The BRIT Awards 2023, London, England — 11 Feb. 2023